If good character education is good education—and I agree with Marvin that it is—then you are holding in your hands a blueprint for good school design. Lucid, research-based, and practical—I recommend this to anyone who cares about the future of our children.

—Angela Duckworth, Rosa Lee and Egbert Chang Professor of Psychology
at the University of Pennsylvania, USA, and author
of *Grit: The Power of Passion and Perseverance*

In *PRIMED for Character Education*, Marvin W Berkowitz unpacks character education in a way to understand our personal responsibility to the future of our societies: the diversity of youth who cross our paths along the K-12 corridor. Through multiple personal and professional examples, he clearly points out to adults the power of our personal presence upon others. Dr. Berkowitz brings decades of teaching and mentoring of K-12 leaders to the academic landscape, and in this book he offers proof that "Character education embraced and lived out lays the foundational requirements for creating a better world."

—Clifton L. Taulbert, President and Founder of The Freemount Corporation
and author of *Eight Habits of the Heart for Educators*

In my last endorsement of his writing, I wrote, "This is Berkowitz at his best." I was wrong. *This* is. The PRIMED framework is one of the most important developments in character education in a long time.

—Thomas Lickona, Director of the Center for the 4th and 5th Rs at SUNY Cortland,
USA, and author of *Character Matters* and *How to Raise Kind Kids*

Marvin Berkowitz has dedicated his life to the flourishing of young people and, in this most recent of books, provides a reliable guide on how to get "PRIMED for Character." Clear, thorough, and readable, this is a very accessible book written from long and tested experience. This book is a must for educators and parents and will stir debate on why character matters so that young people can flourish regardless of what life brings.

—Professor James Arthur OBE, Director of the Jubilee Centre for Character
and Virtues at the University of Birmingham, UK

Marvin Berkowitz is our world's foremost character educator and his new book overflows with useful tools and spot-on ideas. *PRIMED for Character Education* is nothing short of an evidence-based roadmap for educators to help their students understand, care about, and practice the character strengths that will enable them to flourish in school, in the workplace, and as citizens.

—Arthur Schwartz, President of Character.org

I believe that there are no silver bullets or shortcuts in character education. Educators, parents, and children must "do the work" if we are to build a better world in which human goodness can flourish. Having said that, Marvin Berkowitz has spent decades breaking down the code of what this looks like in real, practical terms, and here we have the result. The PRIMED model strikes the difficult balance between academic rigor and user-friendliness, and this book serves as a field guide for anyone in education who wants to make character education happen. Marvin's stories, sense of humor, and simple steps towards character have been transforming schools across the world.

—Henry May, CEO and Co-Founder of Coschool

Based on his knowledge and experience, Marvin Berkowitz probably knows more than anyone about what works, and what doesn't work, in character education at all grade levels. This book is an absolute treasure—a valuable resource for any educator who wants to bring out the best in our young people.

—Hal Urban, author of The Power of Good News

Marvin Berkowitz has spent a lifetime studying and experimenting with best practices that promote what he calls "the flourishing of human goodness." As a psychologist first concerned with enhancing adolescent moral development, he has evolved into the country's premier character education advocate and spokesperson. The PRIMED model he developed grew out of 40 years of his academic investigations, his contacts with educators and thought-leaders throughout the world, and his practical experiences as the director of the gold standard in university-based character education leadership. PRIMED *for Character Education* will become the model for excellence in morally based democratic education and should be widely read by all those responsible for the education of our children.

—Jacques Benninga, Professor of Education of California State University, Fresno, USA

Marvin Berkowitz's PRIMED model combines research, illustrated with solid examples and common sense, to illustrate and inform educators on how they can develop schools that promote excellence for all stakeholders. This book should be required reading for all educators and others who are passionate about how schools can change the lives of students as well as the adults who teach and love them.

—Philip Fitch Vincent, Director of the Character Development Group

PRIMED for Character Education will be a classic. A must-read for every educator, it is a treasure trove of big ideas about character and scores of strategies for principals and teachers. It's an extraordinarily useful text because Marvin Berkowitz gives us the conceptual framework and practical tools to help our students become good people and productive citizens.

—Thomas R. Hoerr, Scholar in Residence at University of Missouri–St. Louis, USA, Emeritus Head of New City Schools, and author of *Taking Social Emotional Learning Schoolwide*

PRIMED for Character Education

In *PRIMED for Character Education*, renowned character educator Marvin W Berkowitz boils down decades of research on evidence-based practices and thought-provoking field experience into a clear set of principles that leaders, administrators, and teacher-leaders can implement to help students thrive. The author's original six-component framework offers a comprehensive guide to shaping purposeful learning environments, healthy relationships, core values and virtues, role models, empowerment, and long-term development in any PreK-12 school or district. This engaging and heartfelt book features tips for practice, anecdotes from award-winning schools, and straightforward tenets from moral education, social-emotional learning, and positive psychology.

Dr. Marvin W Berkowitz is Sanford N. McDonnell Endowed Professor of Character Education and Co-director of the Center for Character and Citizenship at the University of Missouri-St. Louis, USA.

KD 12.21.2022 0835

PRIMED for Character Education

Six Design Principles for School Improvement

Marvin W Berkowitz

Routledge
Taylor & Francis Group

NEW YORK AND LONDON

First published 2021
by Routledge
52 Vanderbilt Avenue, New York, NY 10017

and by Routledge
2 Park Square, Milton Park, Abingdon, Oxon, OX14 4RN

Routledge is an imprint of the Taylor & Francis Group, an informa business

© 2021 Taylor & Francis

Library of Congress Cataloging-in-Publication Data
A catalog record for this book has been requested

ISBN: 978-1-138-49254-7 (hbk)
ISBN: 978-1-138-49255-4 (pbk)
ISBN: 978-1-351-03026-7 (ebk)

Typeset in Utopia
by Apex CoVantage, LLC

I was fortunate to grow up around a group of phenomenal teachers. My mother's college "clique" consisted of five women who were great people and exemplary teachers. One of them, Esther Abramson, was divorced most of her working life and dedicated herself to her calling as a high school mathematics teacher in Stuyvesant High School, a STEM magnet school in New York City. While I knew her as an eccentric loving and charismatic "aunt," I came to learn of her passion and excellence as an educator. I remember my father lovingly teasing her for continuing to teach long after she had qualified for a full pension—pointing out that she was earning less by teaching than the pension would pay. Later, when she was diagnosed with cancer, I went to visit her in her apartment. I noticed a plaque from MIT. Apparently, MIT polled its students about their favorite teachers, and her name came up most often, so they named a scholarship in her honor. Then I spotted a framed certificate from Cornell University. Apparently, something similar had happened there. She had two large filing cabinets full of correspondence from her former students. When Esther succumbed to her cancer, I could not get to New York in time for the funeral, but was able to observe it online live. I witnessed an array of adults who had been her students years, even decades, before, who got up to give testimony to how she had impacted their lives. Esther did more than teach math. In the words of the Canadian author and educator, Avis Glaze, she changed lives . . . for the better. She did that by caring about their character—about the kind of people they would become—and she did *that* by giving priority to their life journeys, building authentic and enduring relationships with them, and investing in a developmental approach that both supported and challenged them in the long run. She did all this in service of nurturing the flourishing of every students' potential for human goodness. I dedicate this book to Esther and to all the other amazing educators from whom I have learned most of what is in the following pages.

Contents ●●●●●

Part I

•••••

Mapping the Terrain
of Character Education

1

●●●●●

To the Point

A book should have a purpose. This book actually has more than one purpose. This book will be about kids, schools, families, human goodness, life's lessons, adult culture, and much more. It will even include aphorisms for life, humor and jokes, magic and fairy dust, passion and humility, and pedagogical faith. We are going to cover a lot of turf.

But the most important and unifying purpose of the book is to shed light on how *we can build a better world by understanding, committing to, and acting upon what is most effective in nurturing the flourishing of human goodness, especially in kids.*

To do so, we will have to explore what we mean by human goodness, why it is important to nurture its development, and most centrally for this book, *how* we can best do that. We will be focusing on the knowing, the being, and doing of character and character education, as we shall see something that is often depicted as the head, heart, and hand of character. We will support the knowing (the head) of what we mean by character and its development and education. We will emphasize the ways we have to be (the heart) with each other and especially students to optimally nurture the flourishing of character. And we will emphasize what we have to do (the hand) as character educators.

To do all this, this book first examines what we mean by character, human goodness, and its development and flourishing. It is necessary to get some level of shared understanding about the central concepts of the book before we venture too far in exploring them and how we can practically make them happen.

Then the book will focus mostly on six big ideas. These ideas are Design Principles for how to nurture the development of human goodness, as well as other parts of human growth and academic learning. I use the acronym PRIMED as a memory aid for them, and I have limited it to just six big ideas to make it more manageable and memorable.

It was a surprise to me that this model has found its way to the core of most of my work with educators. They say they find it helpful and meaningful, and I find it a great way to help them understand what is really most fundamental, not just in character education but in education in general. Furthermore, I have discovered the synergy between such principles for educators and for parents in nurturing the flourishing of goodness in kids (and in people in general, for that matter). Happily, research confirms that what works in families works in schools—and vice versa. The Six Design Principles of PRIMED, which are essential fundamental principles with evidence-based practices, are as follows: *Prioritizing* character in the school; intentionally building healthy *Relationships* among all stakeholders; using *Intrinsic motivators* so students Internalize the core values of the school; *Modeling* the character you want students to develop; *Empowering* all stakeholders to be co-owners and co-authors of the journey; and taking a long-term *Developmental perspective* on the character goals and methods in the school.

As we move through each of the six PRIMED principles, we will take a deep dive into why each one is important, and, even more important, what each looks like in educational practice. Effective practice, grounded in deep understanding, is the heart of this book. My intent is to provide many concrete examples of effective practice, usually from exemplary practitioners who have been there and done it. Through these examples of the six PRIMED principles in action, I hope to inspire and equip educators to begin the daunting journey—or continue that journey if you're already on it!—of personal, professional, and pedagogical transformation.

●●●●●

To Be or Not to Be

For Shakespeare, this was about living or dying, but for PRIMED, it is about *how to live*. How to *be*.

Although this book is about good educational practice, it is much more than an educational manual. It is also a set of guidelines for personal transformation. Many years ago, I realized that effectively supporting the flourishing of human goodness in schools (or families, or anywhere for that matter) is first of all a matter of "being" and then a matter of doing. Parker Palmer emphasized that what we do must flow from our inner core, in other words our character. That character, that "being," not only guides our practice; it is part of our practice. Our doing comes from who we are, our being. Who we are directly impacts those around us.

In my character-focused work with schools, parents, and communities, I find myself saying more and more often, "Character education is a way of being." My friend and colleague Charles Elbot, co-author of *Building an intentional school culture* and an exemplary character educator and educational leader, heard me say that and observed that this is a very Buddhist perspective (Charles is a Buddhist). Charles also pointed me to a set of wonderful quotes from Parker Palmer about "being," quotes worth sharing with you here. In an interview with L.J. Rittenhouse, Palmer said, "Leadership is a matter of how to be, not how to do" and "Education at its best calls us to make an inner journey, not only so we can live better lives, but also to have greater life-giving impact on the world around us." He also has said, "We all know that what will transform education is not another theory, another book, or another formula but educators who are willing to seek a transformed way of being in the world." Therefore, this "one more book" will be a success only if it helps educators transform their ways of being. This new way of being, coupled with deeper knowing, leads to a new way of doing. All too often, people want to jump right to new ways of doing. They do this by asking for methods, curricula, lesson plans, and programs for character education. In essence, they skip right past the critical task of changing oneself as an educator, that is, of transforming one's way of being as foundational to effectively doing.

There is an intimate connection between being and doing to be sure. Aristotle argued that transforming habits (doing) early in life creates the foundation for the later development of virtues (being).

Confucius had a somewhat different but clearly related idea about the relation of being and doing. Michael Puett and Christine Gross-Loh, in their book *The Path*, argue, "We must become aware that breaking from our normal ways of being is what makes it possible to develop different sides of ourselves." This is the path to seeing ourselves "as malleable" (having a growth mindset about ourselves). Confucius even offers a strategy for doing this. We need to be self-reflective and see our current patterns of behavior (especially very minor ones) and then actively work to change those simple patterns by creating better "rituals." In fact, goodness for Confucius was how we *be and do* with others. According to Puett and Gross-Loh,

> Confucian goodness is not something you can define in the abstract. It's the ability to respond well to others; the development of the sensibility that enables you to behave in ways that are good for those around you and draw out their own better sides.

What a great definition of character education! Character education is how we *be* with others and then what we *do* as a consequence, in order to nurture the flourishing of their human goodness. Ideally, our inner character informs our outward living, and our outward living both represents and reciprocally transforms our inner being.

Finally, as a Catholic friend pointed out, this emphasis on who we are "on the inside" as the wellspring of what we do on the outside is also fundamental to the Judeo-Christian view of the human person. Rabbi Harold Kushner, in his book *When All You've Ever Wanted Isn't Enough*, writes: "You don't become happy by pursuing happiness. You become happy by living a life that means something." In the Gospels, Jesus reserved his harshest words for those religious leaders of his day whose pious external actions were done to impress and lord it over others, not out of love of God or neighbor. Christ likened these religious hypocrites to cups that were clean on the outside but filthy on the inside. By contrast, acts of true goodness and holiness come from "the store of goodness" within a person.

All of this is about more than teaching kids in schools. It is a path for living. My friend and colleague Mike Park is the founder of WeBe Schools—a character education program that relies heavily on PRIMED—and is now also the CEO of CharacterPlus, a character education professional development organization in St. Louis Missouri. He has said that he uses PRIMED as a daily meditation for personal improvement, which is much more than I ever envisioned for it.

So the point here is not to artificially separate "being" and "doing" but to call attention to their *relationship*. As we'll see throughout the book, that relationship is bidirectional and dynamic. Our being—who we are on the inside, our hearts and minds, our character—clearly affects our doing. Our doing, in turn, has the potential to transform our being. Character education interventions can capitalize on this bidirectional interaction. Give self-centered teenagers real responsibilities in a face-to-face service learning project where they can see and feel how they are making a difference in the life of a needy child or a vulnerable senior citizen and that experience can, for those teens, change their sense of efficacy, sense of purpose, and moral identity—the very core of their being.

Because character education is first a way of being and then a way of doing—of living our lives—becoming an effective character educator entails changing our way of being, that is, changing who we are and how we engage the world, especially our schools and the kids and adults within them. So, let us look at two metaphors for education and character development and how they fit or do not fit with this notion of education as a way of doing that flows from being and is built upon deep knowing.

● ● ● ● ●

Mechanistic vs. Organismic Metaphors

Often we do not pay close enough attention to what comes out of our mouths. Sometimes our words misrepresent (knowingly or not) how we really think and/or how we tend to act. Other times those words reveal how we think about things whether we are aware of it or not. We will come back to the former problem later.

Now I will focus on a specific contrast in how we can talk about and think about children, human development, and education, whether for character or for anything else. I use the notions of organic vs. mechanical concepts, metaphors, and terminology. So much of what we say and do in education is framed in terms of mechanics. We *teach*. We *transfer* knowledge. We *control* behavior. We *manage* classrooms. We *engineer* school change. And so on.

Instead, I want to hear us talking about and enacting more organic processes. We should *nurture* learning and development. We should *foster* understanding and human flourishing. We should educate for character. Humans are organic entities. Organic wholes, not machines. Human learning and development are better seen through an organic framework and not a mechanical one.

Nor are kids isolated beings. They are embedded in all sorts of interacting social systems: Families, classrooms, grade levels, friendships, peer reference groups, clubs, teams, youth organizations, faith communities, etc. We need to understand these organic systems to which they belong and how those social ecologies function if we want to maximize their power to support the flourishing of human goodness in children, along with their academic learning. When a kid is not "working" right, we cannot simply find the defective part and replace it. We have to look at the totality of that young person's nature and life circumstances and find ways to add nourishment that are likely to lead to a better organic dynamic.

When my son was struggling in adolescence, I realized that what my wife and I were doing was assuming that there was a mechanical "fix." I acted as if there was a large wall covered with an array of knobs, levers, buttons, and dials, each representing some mechanical act we could do, such as changing what we say, creating contingencies for his behavior, teaching him, etc. As a consequence, our job as parents became trying every one and every possible combination of them, believing that eventually we would stumble on the right mechanical solution—flip the right combination of switches while turning the right combination of dials and pushing the right buttons—and all my son's challenges would immediately be solved. What worked was discovering that there was no such quick fix. He had to grow and take at least shared ownership of his challenges. This was part of a complex family (and extra-familiar) dynamic. An organic one. We had to continue to love him. We had to let him know we were there for him. We had to set limits and enforce them. We had to listen. We had to be patient. He had to mature.

There was no mechanical fix, but there was an organic one, because he is not a machine.

Schools make the mechanical mistake all the time. They look for a set of lessons, a curriculum, an assembly on bullying or some other special event that will "teach" character. As we will discover later, this is not how character *develops*.

● ● ● ● ●

Design Thinking

Paul Houston, former Executive Director of the American Association for School Administrators, once said, "Schools are perfectly designed for the results we are getting. If we don't like the results, we need to redesign schools." You can simply swap out the word classrooms for the word schools. The gist of this is that, if we want to redesign schools or classrooms, we have to first redesign ourselves . . . our *way of being*. As

David Brooks, the New York Times columnist and author, wrote, "Social transformation follows personal transformation." It means looking in the mirror and figuring out how you have *to be* different; and then strategically working to make it happen. That is both daunting and difficult to do. My hope is that this book will help.

One way of helping with that self-design challenge is to provide you with a set of aphorisms that I have found to be not only useful but also critical to overcoming the many challenges of becoming an effective agent for nurturing the flourishing of goodness in kids. In a sense, you have already encountered one. Understanding that character education must entail a way of being rather than merely changing our outward practices, our way of doing. When I use the aphorism that character education is more a way of being than doing, what I mean is that changes in doing, in educational practices and strategies, are far less impactful than changes in who you are as a person and educator. Ultimately we want a synergy between being and doing and having it all grounded in a deep understanding (knowing) of character, character development, and character education. Here is a list of the aphorisms we will explore in this book:

- Character education is way of *being*, more than it is a way of doing.
- Look where the keys are, not just where the light is best.
- Character education *is* rocket science.
- *Tikkun Olam* (heal the world).
- Good character education is good education.
- Remember the power of beginnings.
- Excellence is fragile and hard to sustain.
- Every problem is an opportunity in disguise.
- Kids don't care how much you know until they know how much you care.
- Be the character that you want to see in your students.
- Always aim for perfection but never expect it.
- Serenity Prayer (courage to change what you can, serenity to accept what you cannot, and wisdom to know the difference).
- Children do not develop in straight lines.
- Leaders need to lead with their "right."

● ● ● ● ●

Just Joking

Let us frame this entire book with another aphorism. To do that I need to tell you a joke. While jokes can serve many purposes, they are not necessarily merely fluff or entertainment. They can effectively teach. A great example of this, by the way, is Thomas Cathcart and Daniel Klein's book *Plato and a Platypus Walk into a Bar*, which uses jokes and humor to teach philosophy. Here is a well-known joke that helps frame a central purpose of this book.

Finding the Keys to Effective Character Education

A man is walking down the street late at night and sees a second man up ahead, on his hands and knees searching through the grass under the streetlight at the corner. So he approaches him and says, "Did you lose something?" The searcher replies, "Yes, I lost my car keys and can't get home without them." The first man says, "Let me help you", gets down on his hands and knees, and starts to comb through the patch of grass under the street light. It does not take long for it to become apparent that there are no keys in this small patch of grass. So the helper asks, "Are you sure you lost your keys here?" to which the man who lost his keys replies, "No. I lost them about a half a block back that way." The helper, surprised and exasperated, asks, "then why are we looking here?" to which the man who lost his keys replies, "The light is better here."

I find this humorous story to also serve as a helpful aphorism on life and on character education. I constantly encounter educators who are looking where the "light is better" rather than where the keys actually are. I am even willing to say this may be to some extent true of *most* educators, so don't assume it doesn't apply at all to you. I hope you take the time to really think about what this book suggests are the true keys to character development and to ask whether you may have been focusing instead on some of the well-intentioned but ineffective character education practices that are rampant. This kind of self-examination can be personally and professionally very challenging, even threatening, so I will introduce both the keys and the distracting lamp light slowly as we move through the book. However, if you are, as Margaret Wheatley has said, "open to the possibility" and you have some professional humility (and for most of us, humility is a challenging virtue), then you may discover ways that you have been looking under the streetlight and missing where the real keys are. This book is about six keys and where they are "hidden"—though not hard to find if we are looking in the right places.

The challenge to you and all educators is to stop being distracted by the light and instead learn where the keys to character development really are . . . and then go there for guidance on how to effectively *nurture the flourishing of human goodness*. I hope this book will serve as a guide to lead you from the light to the keys.

Amy Johnston was an exemplary character education principal (who led Francis Howell Middle School to recognition as a National School of Character) and since has earned her doctorate in character education and works for Character.org, Character-Plus, and the University of Missouri-St. Louis' Center for Character and Citizenship. She recounts the story of when FHMS first started seeing not only the behavioral and developmental results of thoughtful character education but also the (almost inevitable) corresponding academic gains. Her fellow principals came to her and asked what she was doing to get such impressive academic results. They wanted to replicate it in their schools.

Her answer, "Character education." When they asked, "What do you mean?" she described her school's investment in relationship-building and empowering structures; they did not believe that could be the explanation and said, "What else have you got for me?" It seemed like magic to them. So they walked away, having hoped for a curriculum or an easy-to-replicate change in pedagogy. In other words, they wanted a mechanical fix. However, it was an organic change in the school's "way of being" that resulted in a different way of "doing school," one that prioritized cultivating positive relationships and building positive school and classroom culture. That was the secret of FHMS's exemplary character education success story, including its impressive academic gains.

Here is a similar story. I brought two visiting Japanese scholars to Lindbergh High School, a truly exemplary public suburban high school, both academically and for character. I was concerned about the visit to this school at this time. There had been two principal changes in two years, after a long run of remarkable growth and success under Ron Helms, the leader of this character-based transformation. Having mentored nearly 1,000 school leaders over the past two decades, I knew how disruptive leadership change could be to a school. First there was the disruption of a successor to Ron Helms who did not fit the LHS mission and vision and lasted only a brief time. This made me particularly worried about sustaining the LHS success trajectory. Well, I need not have worried. Eric Cochrane, the next and current principal, not only smoothed over some of the rough spots from the first transition but brought LHS back to the same brilliant path they had been on for over a decade. He had been a teacher there during the early years of the initiative and understood what made it work.

I noticed the different lenses through which my two guests and I were looking for the "keys" to their success. They were focused heavily on academic achievement and the superficial practices of character education. They wanted to be sure that character education did not lessen the academic emphasis. This is ironic, because over a period of 11 years LHS had gradually but steadily ascended to become the top academic high school in the entire state of Missouri and claimed it was mostly due to character education, particularly the empowerment of students. Students at LHS are empowered to mentor other students, generate strategies to increase school-wide academic achievement, authentically design and run school-wide events, propose meaningful school changes, etc.

My guests, however, kept asking about and looking for character lessons and photographing character posters in the hallways. I, on the other hand, was looking for culture, empowerment, and relationships. I was most struck with the autonomy of the students, who appeared to enjoy an impressive degree of freedom and to be using it responsibly. As we walked through the hallways of LHS, there were students everywhere, and this was during class time. Students were moving from one part of the building to another. Small groups sitting in a circle in the hallway working on a project. Individuals in the hallways, laying on the floor drawing a poster or assembling a project or reading or writing. Moreover, no teachers questioned them or ordered them to stop. I did not see evidence of "hall passes." When we asked students what the biggest influence at LHS was that impacted student character, their answer was "empowerment," which is the E in PRIMED and the answer I got from Ron Helms, the founding principal of LHS's character initiative.

Effective character education is not magic. It just seems that way when one looks where the light is better or where the shiny low-impact strategies are. I hope this book will lead you to focus on where the keys to nurturing human goodness really are and how understanding opens the door for impactful transformations first in being and then in doing.

It's been said that there are three kinds of education: Education we do *to* students, education we do *for* students, and education we do *with* students. Effective character education is collaborative, education done *with* students, making full use of our human capital. That requires a different way of thinking and a commitment to different priorities, especially to relationships and the empowerment of all stakeholders—in short, what I've been calling a *different way of being*. From that, comes a *different kind of doing*—practices corresponding to the PRIMED Principles that will truly make a difference in students' development as human beings, the kind of difference we all want to make.

● ● ● ● ●

How This Book Is Organized

This book is organized around the Six Design Principles of the PRIMED framework. It is also organized in eight parts, each comprised of chapters. The first part sets the scene by defining the field of character education, giving some history (Chapters 1 and 2), and arguing for its importance (Chapter 3). Then it introduces PRIMED, with Chapter 4 providing an overview of PRIMED, each element of which is covered in the next six parts.

You can think of the Design Principles as six broad concepts. At the end of each of these parts, you will find a worksheet for school assessment supporting implementation enhancement and strategic planning. You will also find lists of resources for exploring the specific Design Principle of PRIMED in that part.

Part II covers the first concept, Prioritization, which is a bit different from the others and gets more attention (Chapters 5–10). In some ways, it is a meta-element, because it not only signifies prioritizing character education in general, but it also applies to each of the other five elements more specifically. For example, through Prioritization, we want schools to make character education *a* school priority (e.g., putting it explicitly in the School Improvement Plan). However, Prioritization also means that we want schools to prioritize each of the six elements of PRIMED; for example, relationships (the R in PRIMED) and the modeling by adults in the school (the M in PRIMED). We define Prioritization in Chapter 5, but then we turn to the categories of evidence-based practices we identified in our review of the scientific research on character education. These include rhetorical prioritization (Chapter 6), resource allocation (Chapter 7), the role of climate (Chapter 8), school structures (Chapter 9), and the critical role of school leadership (Chapter 10).

Part III covers Relationships. We justify the importance of relationships in Chapter 11. Chapter 12 focuses on building relationships within the school, and Chapter 13 focuses on building relationships with stakeholders external to the school.

Part IV is about supporting Intrinsic Motivation and the Internalization of core character strengths. Chapter 14 explains and justifies a focus on Intrinsic Motivation and internalization. Chapter 15 is a cautionary note about the dangers in relying on extrinsic motivators for character development. Chapter 16 presents the evidence-based implementation strategies for increasing Intrinsic Motivation and the internalization of character strengths.

Part V is about the importance of Modeling for character development. Chapter 17 provides a justification for the importance and centrality of role modeling, especially by significant adults within the school community. Chapter 18 presents implementation strategies for institutionalizing positive role modeling.

Part VI covers Empowerment. Chapter 19 defines empowerment—especially in schools—and justifies the importance of empowerment in character education. Chapter 20 presents the evidence-based implementation strategies of empowerment.

Part VII is the final section on the individual Design Principles and covers Developmental Pedagogy. Chapter 21 explains what it means to take a Developmental Perspective in character education. Chapter 22 presents the pedagogy of how to educate for the long term.

Part VIII is a single chapter (Chapter 23) that ties it all together and closes out the book.

2

●●●●●

Mapping the Terrain

Before we go further in exploring the Six Design Principles of PRIMED and their implementation strategies, we need to explore the key concepts in this book and in the field of character education. This book is centrally about nurturing the flourishing of human goodness in kids. So what do we really mean by that?

●●●●●

The End Game

It is helpful, when thinking about interventions such as character education, to start "with the end in mind." Sometimes this is called "backwards design." The idea is that any effective character education initiative needs to start with a clear understanding of what we are trying to impact. Any journey not only begins with a single step but also needs a destination. Knowing where you are trying to get to is essential for getting there.

It is also important to understand that a destination does not imply a single route. You can, of course, have a road map with specific steps and directions, sort of a Google map or GPS telling you each turn to take to reach your desired destination. It is also like a recipe for which following very specific instructions ideally leads to the desired dish. But character education is more like *being* a chef than like *doing* the recipe.

Charles Elbot, however, points out that, for character education, what we need is a compass rather than just a road map or set of specific directions. We need to know where we are headed, but we can choose the path from among many options. This allows us to adjust and even improvise when we encounter the unexpected. Think of the Six Design Principles as six north stars. Certainly we will be presenting many specific directions to each of them, but they are suggestions or options, rather than required steps.

The impressive new building for the US Air Force Academy's Center for Character and Leadership Development is named Polaris Hall. The idea was to use the North Star as a guiding symbol for its name and its design. Navigators have long used the North Star as a constant guide for keeping their journeys on course. In fact, when you sit in the defendant's chair in the USAFA Honor Courtroom, you are sitting under a magnificent glass ocular tower that always points to the North Star. It is remarkably clever, meaningful, and symbolic. For character education, human goodness serves as the North Star.

However, using a compass does not mean we should be vague about our destination. We may say, "The end is character" or "the end is human goodness," but what is character and what is human goodness? We need to identify our character education goals at some reasonable level of clarity and specificity for them to be our North Stars in designing, implementing, and assessing our character education initiatives. What exactly do you mean when you say you want to "teach character?" What do you mean by "character?" What do we mean by nurturing the flourishing of human goodness?

We are deeply ensconced in the era of educational accountability, and many of us are bruised by it. However, the right kind of accountability is actually a good thing. Knowing what you want to accomplish, figuring out what is most likely to get you there, and having a way of assessing whether it is happening is a . . . well, a good thing. The challenge with the current mania for accountability in education is not those steps but rather the often deeply flawed ways of assessing outcomes and trying to motivate academic achievement through high stakes consequences. This has led to cheating on these high stakes exams and a narrowing of the curriculum to focus heavily or exclusively on only that which is being tested. That is the rotten apple in the accountability barrel. Unfortunately, flawed approaches to accountability are deeply embedded in academic educational practice—and not just in the US—but spreading across the educational face of the planet.

Fortunately, character education has resisted the obsessed-with-test-scores approach to accountability that has caused many schools to narrow the curriculum mostly to reading and math and in the process rob kids of exposure to the arts and other humanizing educational experiences. But it is also true that character educators have neglected accountability to a fault. We have tended not to systematically define outcomes, align practices with research and outcomes, and assess success effectively. There is very little of this kind of accountability in character education, which is a shame. We would be much more effective if we knew concretely what our character outcomes are, were able to define them in measurable ways, knew what research shows nurtures them, and then had valid ways of assessing whether our efforts were actually impacting the flourishing of our specific targeted aspects of human goodness.

So to start at the end, we need to begin with the outcome and address the questions "What is character?" and "what do we mean by human goodness?" Before we do that, we need to take a moment to address the obstacles to even talking about this with clarity and honesty.

● ● ● ● ●

A Word About Words

What is the best term for this field of *nurturing the flourishing of human goodness*? That is precisely my point here. In the past, I have used the terms "semantic morass" and "semantic minefield" to describe the confusing and often treacherous jumble of terms used to identify what are actually vastly overlapping ideas. There are many competing voices and terms: Moral education, character education, values education, virtue education, social-emotional learning, positive psychology, positive youth development, character strengths, etc. Moreover, they tend to vary across cultures and time.

The term character education had a period of ascendency in the late nineteenth and early twentieth centuries in the US, then lost "market share" until it made a comeback in the early 1990s. Now it is competing in a "marketplace" filled with newer terms and movements like social-emotional learning and positive psychology. Yet character education is growing as a preferred term in many places in the world, such as the United Kingdom (thanks in large part to the Jubilee Centre for Character and Virtue and to Character Scotland), Singapore (thanks to the Ministry of Education and its Character and Citizenship Branch), Latin America (thanks in part to an investment by the Templeton World Charity Foundation), and Indonesia (where it seems to be more of a grassroots movement encouraged by political leadership). The point here is that the terrain is bumpy, complex, and variable, across time and location.

Dealing with human goodness and flourishing can be inherently polarizing and even frightening. It ultimately needs to deal with issues of right and wrong, of morality and ethics, which makes people uncomfortable and even suspicious. The idea of schools or even of society "dictating" what is morally right or wrong is off-putting to many people, because it may threaten our deeply held beliefs and feels disempowering and controlling. Consequently, people project their fears on the terms used, regardless of which ones are used. I remember a meeting of educators and educational policy makers interested in character education. In the same room, one person voiced concern that character education was a liberal move to counter traditional religious and cultural values, and another voiced a concern that it is a conservative Christian movement to sneak religious values into liberal public schools.

Common trepidations abound. Whose values will you be teaching? Who exactly are these teachers who will be telling my kid what is moral and what is not? We all have our own morals, who are you to impose yours? This stuff should be taught in faith communities or in families and not in schools. And so on. As we move around the world, some terms are readily acceptable and others are very off-putting. Even in the United States, you will encounter different comfort levels with terms like character education in different places. Right now it is a familiar and acceptable term in Missouri and New Jersey but not in Connecticut, for example.

Therefore, it is necessary to talk about some of these issues here before we go too far in exploring how to educate for human goodness. Only then can we get into the meat of this book, which is looking at where the keys to human flourishing are, avoiding being dazzled and distracted by the streetlights, and learning how to implement those keys to human goodness and flourishing.

● ● ● ● ●

What Is Character?

As you will have noticed already, I have mainly been using two terms: Character education and nurturing the flourishing of human goodness. I am using them interchangeably here. Character education is the common name for this work, but as noted it is one of many competing out there in the culture wars of this field. I have used it for two decades and will stay with it here for multiple reasons. One is historical: The terms "character" and "virtue" have had staying power; they go all the way back to the ancient Greeks such as Plato, Aristotle, and Socrates. A second is conceptual: As I will be using it, character is, in my judgment, the broadest theoretical construct. It subsumes not only school culture development but the other, more specific focuses of fields such as social-emotional learning, service learning, citizenship education, positive education, and the like. The reverse, at least from my perspective, is not true. "Character education" is the biggest tent, encompassing everything I can think of that pertains to this domain of human development.

"Nurturing the flourishing of human goodness," however, is a new term for me, and likely for everyone, because I created it for this book. I am using it as a more cumbersome but more descriptive term. It does not naturally reduce to an acronym (e.g., NFHG). So let us unpack this notion of nurturing the flourishing of human goodness.

My background and training—and entire career for that matter—have focused on the psychological development of morality in humans, mainly children and adolescents, mainly in schools and families. I will return in a moment to defining character and all its components, not merely morality, but it is important to understand that I think morality is the single most important aspect of character.

David Shields, in a 2011 article in the *Phi Delta Kappan*, identified five subcategories of character: Moral, performance, intellectual, civic, and collective. The first four have become central to a number of organizations that are taking leadership roles in character education; for example, The Jubilee Centre for Character and Virtue (UK), the Kern Family Foundation (US), and the Mary Lou Fulton Teachers College at Arizona State University. Some focus exclusively on one category or another. Paul Tough's best-selling book *How Children Succeed* focuses on the performance character strengths that undergird academic success. With support from the John Templeton Foundation, Jason Baehr proposed and in 2013 opened a charter school specifically focused on intellectual virtues: The Intellectual Virtues Academy in Long Beach, California. Others focus on a combination of them. Tom Lickona and Matt Davidson built their 2005 *Smart and Good Schools* model on both moral and performance character. Wolfgang Althof and I, in a 2006 article in the *Journal of Moral Education*, have explored in some depth the interface of moral and civic character. Shields' model is complex, and there are inherent overlaps between some of these aspects of character, which makes it even more challenging to discuss and understand. Let us take a brief look at Shields' four main categories of character.

Moral character consists of those aspects of a person that influence both the inclination and capacity to do what is ethically right. Character.org defines it as "understanding, caring about, and acting upon core ethical values." Elsewhere I have defined it as the set of psychological characteristics that motivate and enable an individual to act as a moral agent. Ultimately, it is about right and wrong and includes knowledge of what is right and wrong, the motivation to try to do what is right, and the skills and other capacities required to act in ways that maximize morality. Moral character involves the knowledge, motives, and competencies that lead to actions that by their nature directly impact the well-being and rights of others.

It is important to note that there are deep philosophical debates about morality and character. One important distinction is between moral character that is defined by one's rights and duties and another that sees it more broadly as also encompassing virtues that go beyond moral obligations, such as humility and gratitude. It is well beyond the scope of this book to resolve such differences, but I will tend to be more inclusive of how I talk about character in general and moral character in particular.

Performance character is about the inclination and capacity to do the best one can at whatever one is doing. This may be an ethical act or an unethical act or something that has nothing to do with right and wrong at all. Ron Berger, as an elementary school teacher in rural Massachusetts, saw a connection between his carpentry work and his profession as a teacher. To do carpentry one needed *an ethic of excellence* (the title of his first book). One would not be willing to make a door that almost closes or a drawer that nearly fits. He wanted his students to develop the same approach to their schoolwork and then to the rest of their lives.

He helped pioneer and refine a brilliant educational approach to make this happen, which he and his colleagues called "project-based learning," which he practiced for 28 years as a teacher, and which he helped to teach others as an educational consultant and author. That pedagogy is now a central part of Expeditionary Learning Schools (eleducation.org) and increasingly used by educators across the country as a way to make learning more meaningful and conducive to character development.

While Ron thought he was mainly focusing on performance character, he soon, however, discovered that he constantly wedded an ethic of excellence to an ethic of goodness, largely because of who he is and his vision for his mission as an educator and a citizen of the world. The projects at the heart of Ron's pedagogy frequently involved students working collaboratively and often rendered service to others. The "culture of craftsmanship" he created in his classroom and the relationships he nurtured with his students and the extended community of the school and small rural town all were important parts of also nurturing moral character as well as performance character. His genius was doing that in a fully integrated way through the experiential classroom projects he had his students engage in. We will explore these particular "keys" later in this book, in the section on Developmental Pedagogy, the sixth Design Principle of PRIMED.

This is probably a good place to make an important philosophical point: As Aristotle used it, "virtue" *meant* "human excellence"—being excellent at *being human*, at being what Aristotle believed human beings are naturally meant to be if they wish to be happy, namely, morally good! In this Aristotelian sense, there is an *intrinsic goodness to excellence*; it is not a separate quality *added on* to goodness.

Civic character consists of the characteristics necessary for effective functioning as a member of society, in the case of most nations where I have worked, a democratic society. Years ago, Wolfgang Althof—former Co-director of our Center for Character and Citizenship—and I defined civic character as "a combination of knowledge about society, skills for participation in society and dispositions to engage constructively in public efforts to promote the common good." John Dewey and, more recently Walter Parker, remind us repeatedly that good citizens do not grow on trees. We have to intentionally socialize and educate them. It is clear that civic character overlaps with the other aspects of character. In fact, there are overlaps between all four of the aspects of character. For example, civic character includes the pursuit of the common *good*, with good including not only what is needed but also what is right. It also entails respect for truth, something we should not take for granted in the current political and cultural climate of "new truth," "alternative truth," etc. Respect for truth is a core element of intellectual virtue. Commitment to the common good includes a respect for human rights, something else we should not take for granted nationally or globally. It is not ethnocentric to argue that civic character is inherently democratic in nature. The form of a political democracy may legitimately vary, but its moral core—a respect for truth and human rights—is essential, not incidental. Indeed, as the Founding Fathers of the United States of America recognized, the primary reason for universal schooling was the cultivation of democratic citizens. Schooling was not viewed by them as career development but rather as citizen development, a perspective that has largely been lost over the last two centuries.

Intellectual character focuses on inquiry. It is concerned with those admirable characteristics of the person that facilitate inquiry. Jason Baehr, a philosopher and founder of the Intellectual Virtues Academy in Long Beach (CA), offers a set of intellectual virtues that include inquisitiveness, reflectiveness, thoroughness, objectivity, impartiality, courage, open-mindedness, humility, and honesty. It should be apparent that such virtues overlap with at least the performance and moral character domains.

So we can see that character is the set of characteristics that motivate and enable one to act as a moral agent (moral character), do one's best work (performance character), effectively collaborate in the common space to promote the common good (civic character), and effectively inquire about and pursue knowledge and truth (intellectual character). These are not discrete domains, but they in fact overlap with each other. This makes understanding, designing, implementing, and assessing character education all the more complex and difficult.

As a psychologist, character and human goodness are multifaceted and complex concepts. But the amateur philosopher in me also sees the point of all this psychological complexity. Human goodness is about ethics and morality, and, as Aristotle so clearly argued over two millennia ago, it is rooted in developing human nature. Human goodness internally is about a set of psychological characteristics, such as one's reasoning and knowledge, one's motives and emotions, one's social and emotional competencies, and one's patterns of behavior. But there is a holism to it as well; that is, it is about the nature of the person. About the kind of person one is. Much of this centers in what we often call one's "self system." This is about one's sense of self. What kind of person do you think you are? What kind of person do you aspire to be? What is the narrative or story you tell yourself—and sometimes others—about your nature, your personality, your life journey? Who do you choose to emulate? Who are your heroes and role models? Do you have a moral compass informing how you live your life? All of this cannot be reduced to one's head, heart, and hands. Rather, it is foundational to the integration of them into your character, your goodness.

But for it to be about "goodness," it has to include a moral compass. I am not a philosopher, so I am always reticent to definitively address what philosophers have tackled for millennia. But I will at least invoke what I learned from Robert Ashmore, an ethical philosopher who was my teacher and colleague at Marquette University decades ago. Morality or ethics must at least be more than self-interest. It has to be focused beyond the self. I would argue that it is partly informed by *Tikkun Olam*. It is trying to make the world a better place for everyone. So human goodness is the set of psychological characteristics that motivate and enable one to be add ethical value to the world. It is the inner inclination to care for and about others and the world in which we all live. It is about deeply and sustainably caring about justice, respect, compassion, and other core ethical goods and acting to promote and safeguard them. In essence it is about the kind of whole person we all want to live near and work with. Human goodness then is the inclination and capacity to make the world a more just and compassionate place for everyone and for that to be central to one's sense of self.

All of this complexity in the nature of character is at the root of why I claim *character education IS rocket science*. Too many educators think character education is simple, and many of the purveyors of character education (e.g., professional organizations, curriculum developers, etc.) send that message; that is, character education is simple and easy. It is not. Some individual practices, like greeting students at the classroom door, may not be rocket science, but the entire enterprise of character education certainly is. I have seen too many well-intentioned educators fumble the character education ball because they did not grasp its complexity and difficulty, usually because they were looking where the light was better and not at the keys of effective character education.

Given my professional focus on moral development, this book will be largely focused on educating for moral character, much more than on civic, intellectual, and performance character. As noted, it is often hard to separate them, and as we'll see, many effective practices develop more than one key in a single stroke.

● ● ● ● ●

Character, Character Development, and Character Education

Having explored the nature of character, it may be helpful to differentiate character from two related terms: Character development and character education. Character is an aspect of the nature of the person, character development consists of the psychological processes that bring about the growth of character, and character education is the intentional nurturing of those developmental processes through the practices of families, schools, and other contexts.

To optimally impact character, ideally for the good although we have to recognize we can cause bad character to form as well, we need to understand its nature and how it develops in the individual. How does one become compassionate or cold-hearted? Where does honesty come from? What are the stages of the development of the capacity to reason about right and wrong, and what supports growth from one stage to the next? Why do some people have strong consciences and others do not? As we look for the keys to character, we need to look not where the light is better but to identify and understand the underlying developmental processes at work.

To engineer epiphanies about character development and education, I have learned to do thought experiments with my audiences. In one of them, I ask the audience to think about one of their own character strengths. I point out that they are not going to share it publicly. We might recognize that we are particularly honest, or unusually compassionate, or highly reliable or responsible, etc. What would you hope that people who know you well would notice about your character and be pleased that you are that kind of person? (Go ahead, take a moment here to pause and do it yourself.)

Once they have settled on a personal character strength, I ask the audience to think about the answer to a second, often much more difficult, question: What made you become that kind of person? Where did that specific character strength come from? Sometimes the source of our character is clear to us. However, it is often not easy to figure out. (Again, stop here and do this yourself.) Then I ask volunteers to share what they figured out or perhaps merely guessed were the sources of their self-identified character strengths.

I have been doing this for many years and have done it with nearly 100 groups around the world. I now know what I will get. As you read the following, compare your reflections with what I hear all the time.

By far the most common answer is that one or both parents had that characteristic and their modeling is what caused you to develop it. The rest of the answers are varying degrees of each of the following: (1) some other significant adult in my life was a role model of that strength; for example, another relative or a teacher; (2) my parents or some other adult had a character weakness that was the opposite of my strength and I swore I would never end up like them; (3) a serious life trauma or challenge either helped me discover a strength within me that I did not know I had, or forced me to develop this strength by necessity to deal with my circumstances; (4) i decided to make my character a self-project and intentionally worked to be a certain kind of person. #4 often is in response to #2 or #3. In other words, our signature character strengths come from adult models (both good and bad), personal goal setting about character, and the necessity to deal with challenging circumstances. Some folks invoke religion as a source of their character. When pressed to explain how religion impacts their character, it often comes to membership in a community with clear shared values.

In our review of parenting for character, John Grych and I not only found evidence of parental role-modeling, but we also identified supported high expectations, focusing on the impact of one's actions on others, love, and empowerment of children as effective at nurturing different aspects of character. All of these have also been found to work for educators.

These are the keys. This is where the keys to character development are. So let us compare these keys to a list of what I have never heard in reply to my thought experiment. No one has reported that his or her signature character strength came from a poster. Nor that it was inspired by a pithy or clever quote about character. No one has reported that their character came from a character lesson in school. Nor from a lecture about character. Nor from a character-focused curriculum. I have yet to hear anyone tell me that their character came from a character award that they or someone else received. I have yet to learn about the power of a character assembly in school where they or others were recognized for good character. And I am still waiting to hear a testimonial about the transformational power of singing songs about character.

No one, anywhere in the world, ever told me that their character strength came from any of those influences. Those are where the light is better, not where the keys are. Unfortunately, those are where educators most commonly go to find the magic of character education. They are not, however, where the real keys to character education are. That is what I will attempt to point out and correct in this book. What I want most fervently is for you to recognize and go to where the keys are.

It is important to note that many of these "non-keys" strategies can be helpful as reminders of what we consider to be good character outcomes and goals. The problem comes when one thinks those reminders themselves nurture the flourishing of human goodness; in other words, that they themselves are the keys.

●●●●●

Espoused Theory vs. Theory in Action

So if modeling, overcoming challenges, taking personal responsibility for one's character development, and other influences we will explore later are the main sources of character development, what is character education? Well, what is widely practiced and what ought to be are sadly two different things. Many years ago, Character.org did a survey of character educators and asked two questions: (1) what is good character education? and (2) what do you do to educate for character? You would expect the answers to be similar. Nope. The answer to question one was an enlightened list of keys; that is, of effective practices. At the top were positive school climate, healthy relationships, role modeling, etc. At the bottom were rewards and recognitions.

The answer to question two, however, was the inverse of the answer to question one. At the top of what they reported doing were the bright lights of the street lamp; i.e., rewards, lectures, and recognitions. Least utilized were exactly the things they said were most effective (relationships, school climate, etc.). It seems they knew intellectually where the keys were, but, when it came to implementation, they ran to the street light.

The gap between what we say and what we do turns out to be a very common human phenomenon, observable in many different contexts. Chris Argyris and Donald Schoen, represented in a series of books between 1974 and 1996, made the distinction between "theory in action" and "espoused theory." While they were more focused on the corporate world, it applies equally well to education. *Espoused theory* is about what you say about how you and the world work. *Theory in action* is about the theory implied in your actions and choices. Many schools may espouse the importance of nurturing a prosocial school climate, of adults modeling good character, and of intentionally nurturing healthy relationships (all parts of PRIMED), but when you look at what they do to foster character development, they load on the bright lights such as assemblies, rewards, recognition, lectures and lessons, and curricula. That is their theory in action. Sometimes they are not even aware of the discrepancy.

How often have we seen schools espouse being loving and nurturing communities and having draconian behavior management systems? Often an educator will espouse an enlightened theory of child development and then resort to behaviorist strategies that treat the child as a pet animal to be constrained and trained, all while authentically loving and wanting the best for kids. And not seeing the contradiction.

This happens in relationships among adults as well. Candidates for school leadership positions often talk a good game during the job interview. A colleague at another university says the candidate hired to be the new Dean of the School of Education spoke eloquently during the interview about the importance of collaborative decision making, working closely with faculty. But after this person was dean, top-down decision making was much more common than collaboration. We might ask, why does sort of thing happen time and again?

There are several possible reasons. One is that there was not a sincere intention to put espoused theory into action. Or the person may be largely unaware of the gap between his or her espoused values and operative values. Or people might wish to act on the espoused theory but don't have an adequate skill set to do so. Often it happens that educators mistakenly believe that the practices they are using do constitute effective implementation of the espoused theory, when in fact they do not.

Finally, and this is all too common, we want to put our espoused theory into more consistent practice, but environmental conditions get in the way. A classroom teacher believes class meetings and cooperative learning foster important aspects of character development but feels there's not enough time because of pressures to cover the curriculum. A principal would like to make relationship building, student empowerment, and building a strong professional community higher priorities, but there are different priorities coming from central office. We often hear educators say, "We'd like to spend more time on character education, but . . ." Often, a mix of all of the above factors keep us from being our best and doing our best to nurture the flourishing of human goodness.

Character education is quite simply the intentional implementation of strategies designed to foster the development of character. Saying that is the easy part. Understanding what will effectively foster character development in schools (and other youth socializing institutions, including families) is a much more complex chore and will be the focus of most of the rest of this book.

Whatever the obstacles to pursuing that crucial goal, this book is about (1) improving our espoused theory of character education by providing evidence of the major psychological influences that nurture the growth of goodness and (2) giving nuts-and-bolts advice about effective implementation practices so that our actions match what good theory tells us we should be doing.

3

•••••

Making the Case

So why should you even care about character education? It may be helpful to learn four things, to help you better understand why I focus on nurturing the flourishing of human goodness.

•••••

Why Do I Dedicate My Career to Nurturing the Flourishing of Human Goodness?

In two words: *Tikkun Olam*.

This is a Hebrew phrase meaning to heal the world. There is an ancient origin story that says that when God created the world, the materials used were taken from large crocks (which is where food and other materials were stored in those days) and that some of them were damaged in the process of creation. Therefore, God charged humans with restoring the damage done in the act of creation. This parable offers a great moral mandate to all of us. We should engage the world and we should live our lives in ways that are most likely to leave it a better place because of our how we lived while in it. That is one way we should *be* in the world.

My leverage point for *Tikkun Olam*, for healing the world, is as a psychologist who specializes in the development of children and adolescents, especially their moral development. By working to improve how we nurture the flourishing of human goodness in children and adolescents, I can contribute to healing the world.

After all, we cannot create a moral world without moral people. As it says at the beginning of Tom Lickona's book *Raising Good Children*, "A child is the only known substance from which a responsible adult can be made." There simply is no future without children, and there is no moral future without moral children. This book is a recipe for how we can heal the world by nurturing the moral development of children, and helping them carry the torch of *Tikkun Olam* in turn by being more disposed to heal the world as well.

Do I believe in progress, decline, or randomness?

I am a long-haul optimist. I think that the history of the human species has been one of long-term moral progress. There are two books that most influenced this view for me. The first was *The History of Childhood* written by Lloyd DeMause in 1974. It traces the history of human conceptions of childhood, child development, and the corresponding ways of treating and parenting children. It was a clear journey from cold, harsh, even cruel and violent treatment of children in European Medieval times (and in US Colonial times) to more and more enlightened and compassionate treatment. The second was Steven Pinker's 2011 book *The Better Angels of our Nature*. It presents a historical analysis of violence in the Western world, showing that violence has consistently declined over thousands of years. We are consistently growing less violent.

Now these two—and related—arguments work only if you pull back the lens and look at long sweeps of time. Certainly, the closer in you focus, the more you can see variability. Human moral evolution needs to be seen over long sweeps of time. Ask yourself this: When more than 100 years ago would you rather have lived? Think about health, safety, longevity, the rule of law, human rights, power distribution, etc. The answer is, "Never." That is particularly poignant if you are a child, a woman, a member of a minority group, elderly, poor, have a disability, etc. Martin Luther King, Jr. said it most succinctly, "The arc of the moral universe is long, but it bends toward justice" in his paraphrasing of the nineteenth-century American abolitionist minister, Theodore Parker. President Barack Obama so loved Reverend King's quote that he had it woven into a rug displayed on the floor in the Oval Office of the White House.

Of course, there are real human weaknesses at play all around us, and they need to be addressed directly in their current forms. However, they do not mean that we are all going to hell in a handbasket. They just mean we remain, as we always will, imperfect, and there is room to improve.

Character education is not about desperation or panic. It is not a last resort or the proverbial finger plugging the leak in the dike. It is not a tourniquet or a last chance. It is an eternal human obligation and endeavor. And it is certainly not a short-term goal or quick fix. Being our best selves means caring about the future and in being part of making a better future more possible and real.

Heraclitus, the classic Greek philosopher who lived over 2,500 years ago, said that "Good character is not formed in a week or a month. It is created little by little, day by day. Protracted and patient effort is needed to develop good character." Like a fine wine, goodness, whether within a person's lifetime or over the longer haul for the human species, takes time and thoughtful, deliberate care. *Tikkun Olam* tells us that it is the obligation of all human beings to dedicate themselves to this eternal project.

My friend and colleague, Bill Puka, a philosopher, once described what he called "developmental love." He defined it as loving a person in a way that maximizes their optimal development. Love people by doing what is in their best developmental interests. According to Aristotle (who lived about a century after Heraclitus), flourishing is the highest achievement of human development (he called it Eudaimonia). Flourishing, for Aristotle, is the full development of moral virtues. Combining Puka, Heraclitus, and Aristotle leads us to the notion of developmental love as the commitment to the possibility and gradual development of the full complement of moral virtues. We will explore this further when we discuss Developmental Pedagogy, the sixth Design Principle of PRIMED.

Progressive or Conservative?

For me these concepts load on whether one emphasizes or orients toward positive change or toward protecting the status quo. Conservative means to conserve, to preserve, and keep as it is. It is a focus on what is and tries to protect that. Sometimes that is a focus on appreciating and preserving what is good in the world, and at other times it is inertia toward avoiding change. Progressivism, on the other hand, focuses more on what could be better and then tries to make the world move in that direction. Of course, there is much that deserves preserving, so this is a matter of orientation and degree. The trick is to not settle, to want to keep moving that arc of history toward justice and other goods, and to not throw the baby out with the bathwater in doing so but rather to preserve that which deserves it. Because I have a growth mindset and because I am a long-haul optimist, I believe that progress is not only possible but a noble goal, and that over the long haul it is likely inevitable. However, our values, goals, and actions can impede its progress or speed it up. It is up to us.

My friend Clifton Taulbert, author of many autobiographical books including *Once Upon A Time When We Were Colored* and *Eight Habits of the Heart*, has often inspired me to reflect on the notion of progressivism. He strongly believes in a growth mindset, in large part because he grew up a poor rural cotton-farming African-American child in the Mississippi Delta during legal segregation and became an educated and highly successful businessperson, author, speaker, Airman, and consultant. Part of his story is the people who populated his childhood and who did not see him as he was but rather saw the possibilities in him. They could have through a fixed mindset seen him as destined to be poor, uneducated, and discriminated against. They did not. They saw what he could become and then invested in those possibilities, even though the world around them said it was not possible and not acceptable.

An interesting sidebar on whether one sees a glass as half full or half empty is what you think about the empty half of the glass. Do you see it as wasted space or as an opportunity? We all have empty parts in our glasses. Do we see the possibilities in them?

Many great entrepreneurs do the latter. In fact, Sir John Templeton, who in my field—and many others—is known as a great philanthropist who invested heavily in supporting character education, made his fortune as an investor who saw opportunities where others did not. He looked for the unnoticed opportunities for growth, and his philanthropic foundations continue to do so.

I recently heard an interview with Father Greg Boyle who provides hope to gang members in Los Angeles by seeing the possibilities in them. Rather than seeing such kids as "at risk," he sees them as "at opportunity."

Cliff Taulbert often reminds us that we should not see children as they are but rather see the possibilities in them. Then we have to, as Sir John Templeton, and Robert Kern, and Sandy McDonnell, and Richard Pieper, and Stephen Bechtel Jr., and E. Desmond Lee, and many other great philanthropists came to do, invest in those kids, those possibilities, and their character.

Character development is not only about individual development. It is also about world building and *Tikkun Olam*.

Localist or Universalist

As a developmental psychologist, I tend to think about fundamental human nature and look for universal processes of development. So I tend to see the commonalities across all children. Not everyone does that.

A couple of years ago, I was reading papers by my graduate students, almost all of whom were teachers who were working toward their principal certification. Most of them worked in urban, under-resourced schools, with under-resourced minority students. What struck me was the frequent skepticism of these experienced educators about effectively doing character education with "these kids." Even more disturbing was that those educators who were themselves from the same minority, under-resourced communities were even more skeptical than were the privileged white educators. They felt that you had to "be" or "do" differently with "these kids," who in their perception would not respond as positively to the character education strategies that had reportedly worked with more "advantaged" kids (from less troubled homes, neighborhoods, etc.). Fortunately, in this class we required site visits to exemplary character education schools from a mix of demographic groups and communities.

We sent them to Premier Charter School, an urban prekindergarten to eighth grade charter school whose students are selected by lottery from within the City of St. Louis.

We sent them to Busch Middle School, a magnet school for character education in the St. Louis Public Schools, the large urban district in the city of St. Louis. We also sent them to Northview High School, a special education high school that serves the county of St. Louis. Seeing impressive character education initiatives and the results of them with what are usually considered more challenging student populations (indeed, the populations they were skeptical about) often opened their eyes to the possibility of effective character education with all kids, including "these kids."

When I take educators to schools or show them videos of schools that do not look like theirs, with kids who do not look like their students, regardless of what the differences may be, I implore them in advance not to see the differences and conclude that what they see will not map on to their worlds. I implore them to not let the shutters come down and or turn off the channel.

Instead, I ask them to look past what does not seem to apply and look for what could apply. What are these schools doing that you *could* adopt or adapt?

In so many fundamental and critically important ways, kids are kids. I work all over the world, and I find that the Six Design Principles of PRIMED apply similarly everywhere. Self-determination Theory tells us that all kids (indeed all people) have three fundamental needs, sometimes called the "ABCs" of human needs: (1) autonomy—to have some control over their lives; (2) belonging—to be cared and about and a member of a community; (3) competence: To be valued and feel that one makes a meaningful contribution. Human beings are much more likely to flourish, to achieve their full potential, when these three needs are met.

Let me say more about the concept of mindset. This is a common term now in education thanks to the work of Carol Dweck in her book *Mindset*. Dweck and her colleagues distinguish between a "fixed mindset" and a "growth mindset." The former assumes that things are unlikely to change, and the latter sees great possibilities for change, especially positive growth. In fact, research says that one way to help under-resourced kids, who tend to have lower rates of school success, to succeed is to change the mindsets of . . . their parents. Really. If their parents come to believe their kids can do well in school, then the kids are more likely to.

Not surprisingly, the mindsets of educators about kids are even more important for kids' success in school. A now classic and groundbreaking study in education by Richard Rosenthal and Lenore Jacobson, described in their 1968 article entitled "Pygmalion in the classroom," demonstrated this powerfully. They told teachers that the results of an intelligence test they administered could reveal which kids were about to take a leap forward in IQ. They then assigned high scores to some of the kids, purely at random, and told the teachers that these kids were about to make a jump in intelligence. Astonishingly, over two years those randomly selected kids did indeed increase in IQ, much more so than did the other kids in the class. Teacher expectations and beliefs, their growth or fixed mindsets, about kids, really matter. Rosenthal and Jacobson called this phenomenon "The Pygmalion Effect."

What Rosenthal's study tells us is that all teachers should have growth mindsets about all kids. His study was about IQ, but we can say the same for character development. After all, one of the most replicated findings in research on teaching and parenting is that having high expectations for kids is a powerful influence on their academic growth and character development. This, too, is part of PRIMED.

Character education is for all kids. Because every kid can—and will—change, and all deserve the chance to flourish and be their best selves.

This is why I do not justify character education, as is so commonly the case, by listing modern ills and stating or implying that the current state is worse than ever. It is not. It can certainly look that way if you cite only statistics that currently are declining (e.g., rising suicide, gun violence, etc.) and/or look at relatively short periods (e.g., years or decades).

Instead, I prefer to justify this project not as a Band-Aid or tourniquet for current wounds—although in the spirit of *Tikkun Olam* we can hope it will help to heal current ills—but as an eternal project of the human spirit. It is about making the best world we can by making the best people we can. As Lickona noted, "A child is the only known substance" from which we can do that.

4

●●●●●

PRIMED

I spend a lot of time advising and mentoring graduate students in education and psychology, most of whom do a large project such as a master's thesis or doctoral dissertation. They hear me, repeatedly, asking for their "logic model," sometimes called a "causal model." Its purpose is to show, typically with a diagram, the logic of cause-and-effect relations among the variables being depicted. I have to thank my colleague Roger Weissberg, founding Director of the Collaborative for Academic, Social and Emotional Learning (CASEL), a psychologist and thought leader for social-emotional learning (SEL), for turning my eye toward the importance and usefulness of logic models.

There are many versions of what a logic model is or should be. For me it is a clear and concise explanation, usually with a graphic representation, of the logic of one's thinking about the relations among the factors assumed to be affecting a particular outcome or set of outcomes. In my case, most of my students are studying or designing educational interventions. Their logic models should state their (1) desired outcome goals (remember "Backward design"?); (2) their intervention strategies (what they propose to do to produce those outcomes); and (3) the relations between the two sets, including a convincing justification of why the interventions should be expected to result in the desired outcomes.

Let me give an actual example. A few years back I encountered a high school principal who had graduated from my yearlong Leadership Academy in Character Education (LACE). He was excited to tell me about his new character education initiative but first wanted to tell me why they were emphasizing character education throughout their school.

They had caught a group of students cheating on exams. This had motivated some teachers to research high school cheating and academic integrity. No doubt they found the Center for Academic Integrity at Clemson University a great resource. Likely they discovered much to their chagrin that academic dishonesty at colleges and high schools is prevalent, even epidemic. Rather than keeping their heads in the sand, they decided to tackle this problem head on.

The principal then described their solution to the cheating. They decided to commit to mastering and implementing service learning and to do so in a comprehensive and thoughtful way. They investigated it, identified resources, and invested heavily in high-quality professional development for their staff. They designed a comprehensive school-wide adoption and integration of service learning. The thoughtfulness and depth of their commitment and implementation impressed me, and I told him so. After all, service learning is an excellent evidence-based educational strategy that repeatedly demonstrates significant positive impacts on both learning and character development.

But I posed this challenge, "What does service learning have to do with academic integrity?" Whereas research on service learning shows many positive outcomes, to my knowledge no research had shown academic integrity to be an outcome of service learning.

They never really had a logic model. They had a desired outcome: Reduction in cheating. They had an implementation strategy: Service learning. But they had no logical connection between them and had never considered the question of cause and effect between their chosen implementation strategy (service learning) and their targeted outcome (academic integrity). They were looking where the light was better, not where the keys to academic integrity were. In this case, the bright light of service learning is in fact a key, just not a key to the door they were trying to open.

Now it is certainly not bad that a high school adopted a high-quality comprehensive implementation of service learning. All schools probably should. It is just a shame that it was like eating a balanced diet to heal a broken leg. General nutrition helps with lots of things, but it will not heal broken bones.

This is common in education in general and character education in particular. This book is about understanding where the keys to character education are and how to implement them effectively. To do that, the rest of this book will examine the six keys or Design Principles that PRIMED represents.

There is plenty of lamentation about the lack of transfer of scientific knowledge in education in general. This means that valuable theory and research about education does not adequately drive practice. Educators either do not know the theory or research or simply do not put it into practice. Sometimes the blame falls on the scholars who either fail to let the world of educational practice know of their theories and research or do so in ways that are simply not intelligible to or manageable by educational practitioners. Sometimes the blame falls on the practitioners who do not care about, consume, or focus on the theories and research data that can shed meaningful light on effective educational practice. Sometimes they rely on intuition instead of logic or data. Sometimes they are simply closed-minded.

A classic example in the field is values clarification. Values clarification was a wildly popular approach to exploring values in schools in the 1960s. It was a good example of the bandwagon effect in education, where educators gravitate enthusiastically to an untested approach. Values clarification was quickly criticized for its philosophy of ethical relativism (there are not universal bases for judging right and wrong), its developmentally inappropriate lessons (life-and-death dilemmas for elementary school children), and finally its lack of evidence of effectiveness. Ultimately research demonstrated that it did not achieve its goals, and it withered away almost as quickly as it had burst upon the educational landscape.

●●●●●

A Step Toward Finding Out What Works

Nearly 20 years ago, Melinda Bier and I proposed to review the existing research on effective character education. No one had yet done that in a systematic way. Thanks to funding from the John Templeton Foundation, we produced *What Works in Character Education (WWCE)*. WWCE uncovered 69 scientifically valid studies of character education and then looked for patterns both in outcomes (what did character education impact?) and methods (what were the most commonly used practices in the effective implementations?). This work guided many practitioners and policy-makers to utilize effective practices, and it still does.

In the ensuing two decades, we have updated the research because there are many new studies and others have begun to review the body of existing research. The National Academies of Sciences, Engineering and Medicine invited us to write a more current review for a "Workshop on Approaches to the Development of Character" funded in large part by the Steven Bechtel, Jr. Foundation (most of the papers from that meeting have subsequently been published in two issues of the *Journal of Character Education*). In writing this paper, Melinda Bier, Brian McCauley, and I decided not only to identify the current list of evidence-based effective practices for character education but also treated the six Design Principles of PRIMED as "cubby holes" into which we sorted the long list of effective practices as examples of each particular Design Principle.

That is the organizational scheme for the rest of this book. I will take each Design Principle in turn—first explaining and justifying it—and then describe the various evidence-based practices that exemplify it, along with cases and anecdotes and resources to support many of the individual practices. I hope this will be both a conceptual guide (PRIMED) and a practical manual (the particular practices corresponding to the PRIMED Principles), so that more educators and schools will be implementing . . . well . . . What Works in Character Education.

● ● ● ● ●

Branding PRIMED

My friend and colleague Mike Park is a marketing and branding expert and a big fan of the PRIMED framework. He suggested that the P in PRIMED, which stands for Prioritization, can be understood as having two meanings. First, it is about making character education an authentic priority in the school. Second, it signifies specifically making each of the other five Design Principles in PRIMED themselves priorities for effectively implementing character education. Hence, all should be capitalized, but the P should be larger. So . . . PRIMED.

● ● ● ● ●

Overview of PRIMED

I listed and briefly described the Six Design Principles of PRIMED at the beginning of the book, but let me briefly review them here. PRIMED represents six fundamental Design Principles of effective character education. They are not specific practices but much broader points of focus. The specific practices are located within the six principles.

As noted earlier, the P in PRIMED stands for Prioritization. It is about making character education in general—and the other five Design Principles in particular—authentic priorities in all a school does and is.

The R is for Relationships, which are the building blocks, the elements, of both good schools and, more specifically, character education and development. Those relationships need to both be intentional and exist between and among all stakeholders in the school.

The I is for Intrinsic Motivation. If character education is to be effective it must become an internal motivation of the person for its own sake and not because it leads to a reward or public recognition. Therefore, the I could also stand for Internalization, that is, getting those desired character outcomes to move from the school to inside the child as a foundational part of who that child is. It becomes an authentic part of the child's way of being in the world.

Table 4.1 PRIMED: Six Design Principles for Effective Character Education

Prioritization	Making educating for character development an authentic and salient **Priority** in the mission, vision, policy, and practice of the school
Relationships	Intentionally and strategically nurturing healthy **Relationships** within and across all stakeholder groups
Intrinsic Motivation	Nurturing the internalization of character and the **Intrinsic motivation** to be a person of character and avoiding extrinsic motivators
Modeling	All adults and other role **Models** embody and exemplify the character that they want to develop in students
Empowerment	Creating a culture and governance structure that **Empowers** all stakeholders, by inviting their voices, listening to those voices, and seriously considering what they have to say, so that each one has the possibility of making a significant difference
Developmental Pedagogy	Takes a **Developmental** perspective in its educational philosophy and practice by educating in ways that support the long-term learning and character development of students

The M is for modeling. Schools need to be sure that all school personnel and all other adults such as parents and community members who come into the building or work with students in other ways exemplify the character the school wants to develop in students. This also includes peer role models, such as older students. The same goes for the school culture and the practices that make it up. Everything sets an example, for good or for ill.

The E is for Empowerment. Schools are where we prepare future citizens who will sustain and strengthen our democracies. Our children will not be prepared for the demands of citizenship if they never experience the democratic process and the responsibilities of being contributing members of society. Unfortunately, schools tend to be more like benevolent dictatorships than democracies. Moreover, if we want to fulfil the fundamental human need for autonomy—including the belief that we can affect the course of our lives and positively impact the world around us—we need to make space for our students' voices now.

The D is for Developmental Pedagogy (or Developmental Perspective). As noted, children and their character develop slowly. As a kindergarten teach once said, "It takes a lot of slow to grow." We need to design our schools and educational practices with an eye toward long-term developmental outcomes and recognize that some practices support long-term human development and others do not and actually may subvert it.

As we examine each of these six Design Principles in depth, we will identify sub-categories, and, within all of them, we will identify specific evidence-based practices. The rest of this book will do just that, one Design Principle at a time.

Each of the following sections, representing each of the Six Design Principles of PRIMED, will have a similar structure. Essentially, the Design Principle will be explained and then the evidence-based practices for how to implement that particular Design Principle will be presented and explained. An overview of the Six Design Principles is presented in Table 4.1. The specific information about each Design Principle is at the end of the respective section in the form of a self-assessment worksheet.

Part II

●●●●●

PRIMED Principle 1: Prioritization

5

●●●●●

What Does It Mean to Prioritize Character Education?

In the video about Francis Howell Middle School's journey to character education excellence, Principal Amy Johnston says, "and you know, they may not be stellar in science, communication arts, and math, but if they are stellar in character, you have done your job." And she meant it. She put character first at her school.

What surprised many of Amy Johnston's school leader colleagues, however, was that putting character first not only led to impressive gains in character and behavior, but it also led to impressive gains in "science, communication arts, and math." Her school pulled far ahead of the district's other middle schools in state academic test scores . . . precisely because she authentically prioritized students' character development.

In a similar spirit, principal Kristen Pelster, after taking the helm of Ridgewood Middle School, asked candidates for teaching positions only about relationships and classroom management and never about content expertise. Character and culture were her priorities because she knew that they were the paths to school success. Her school went from a nightmare (many behavior problems and low academic indices) to a dream (dramatic improvements in behavior and academic achievement).

Despite the oft-perceived tension between focusing on academic achievement and focusing on character development, there is strong evidence of the synergy between these two purposes of education. I like to say, "Good character education is good education." Jack Benninga and I studied 120 California elementary schools and found that more emphasis on character education was related to higher state test scores. We found many studies in our *What Works in Character Education* research review showing the same thing. The Collaborative for Academic, Social and Emotional Learning (CASEL) has done multiple large reviews of research showing this too. CharacterPlus (a St. Louis regional character education organization) has multiple large studies to show their *CharacterPlus Way* model has both character and academic benefits. The list goes on.

The evidence is clear that "good character education is good education" and that prioritizing character education does not detract from academic success. On the contrary, it significantly enhances it.

The Developmental Studies Center (now transformed into the Center for the Collaborative Classroom) did a set of studies of their exemplary Child Development Project (now Caring School Community program). In different regions across the United States, they found wide-ranging and sustained positive impacts on both character and academics. However, they also found that their comprehensive character education practices (such as class meetings, cooperative learning, developmental discipline, building schoolwide community, and involving parents) had those beneficial effects *only if students came to perceive their classrooms and schools as caring communities.* Student perceptions that their schools and classrooms are caring communities are both a result of character education and a mediator of character education's positive impact on other desirable outcomes. When kids feel safe, that they belong, and that others have their best interests at heart, they come to value and bond with their schools. Kids who bond with their schools perform better academically and socially. They pay attention. They do not disrupt. They work harder. Moreover, they have higher aspirations for and expectations of educational success, an important dimension of a growth mindset.

In hindsight, all this seems obvious. If kids come to school fearing bullying, feeling like a cog in a wheel, perceiving adults as more like wardens than nurturing teachers, then they cannot focus as well and do not commit as fully to the hard work of being a student. It is important to emphasize that kids who feel unsafe (and by unsafe we always mean in a range of ways such as physically, emotionally, culturally/racially, and intellectually) there is much more at stake than just academic success. As the educational philosopher Joanne Freiberg (personal communication) so clearly and compellingly puts it,

> Children who are growing up in abusive, neglectful or permissive environments . . . live or die, literally, on how safe, writ large, the environment is for them. If these children do not experience high expectations with the support necessary to meet them, they will become the statistics we are trying to avoid. . . . Children experiencing trauma, including racial trauma in their homes and communities (as well as children who never hear the word, "no," and do anything they want) need to experience a different and better *normal*. They need respite from those environments so that they, too, can thrive.

When the psychologist Angela Duckworth, in her best-selling book *Grit*, talks about the character quality of grit as a path to higher achievement, most people think that just means to work harder and persevere longer. However, Duckworth's definition of grit is *perseverance with passion*. In other words, kids need to be passionate about schoolwork, and that means they need to be motivated to work hard and persevere. Creating a culture of trust and safety and compassion is a very strong motivator. Indeed, it is the "heart" of the *being*—and ultimately the *doing*—of character education.

I often tell principals that I can raise their academic test scores simply. Just get the students to sincerely try harder on the testing day. Get a good night's sleep, have a hearty breakfast, and come to school eager to do well on the test, and then focus and work hard to do your best on the test. However, to get them actually to do that, they have to love the school. Now that is probably true and relatively easy to achieve with most of the little ones. They likely already do. So you just say, "Hey guys, we all love good old Mickey Mantle Elementary School don't we?!" (Sorry, I grew up a New York Yankees fan, and Mickey was *the* Yankee). "So come on in tomorrow and try your hardest on the test, because it really matters to good old MMES!" And chances are most of them will.

But try that with almost any adolescent in middle and high school. Good luck with that. The data suggest that adolescents feel less than amorous about their schools—and for good reason; so many middle and high schools are not structured to help students flourish. At a time in their lives when they need more, not less, active engagement, classes often make them largely passive learners who have to listen to teachers talk at them most of the day. However, if you do effective character education well, such as by following the Six Design Principles of PRIMED, even teenagers are likely to enjoy school, perhaps even emotionally bond to or love their schools.

We have chronicled Ridgewood Middle School (RMS) elsewhere including in a full-page article in *USA Today*, so I will not go into details here. Suffice it to say, through character education RMS went from a failing-in-every-respect school to a National School of Character in only six years. In the process, their percentage of students meeting state standards went from 7% in math and 30% in communication arts to about 70% in each. One of the biggest changes they made was to prioritize character education. An interesting sidelight is that the administrative team of Tim Crutchley and Kristen Pelster intentionally did not even use the term "character education" during the first three years but just went about crafting a new way of being that was relational and trusting and child-centered. Then they named it.

One can make a parallel argument about the adult culture. When staff like working in their school, feel like part of a positive adult community, and trust their principal and each other, they work harder and care more about students and about educating them. Because the leader is modeling all this for and with the staff, they in turn tend to do similar things that nurture the flourishing of human goodness in students, which also helps them succeed academically. Anthony Bryk and Barbara Schneider's book *Trust in Schools* clearly shows that the degree of relational trust among the staff increases the academic achievement of students.

This is another good example of how the keys to school success and student flourishing may not be where you expect to find them. Many people would not look at adult culture at all as being central to character education and certainly not the key to increasing academic achievement. But that is where we keep finding, again and again, one of the most dependable keys to nurturing the flourishing of human goodness in our students and their academic success.

In short, character education and academic teaching are not part of a zero sum game, where one is achieved only at the expense of the other. There is indeed "room on the plate" for both. A saying often quoted by committed character educators turns out to be true; the "character education is not something else on the plate . . . it IS the plate." It is the solid foundation that everything else is built upon.

Focusing on character education is not only a moral obligation (*Tikkun Olam*) and not only an eternal progressive human project. It also supports the other primary purpose of schooling, academic learning.

•••••

Authenticity

There are two ways to consider the challenge of authenticity in character education. The first is to ask whether character education is a primary priority (ideally *the* primary one) or a "derivative" priority. Is its value intrinsic or because of something else it causes or tends to be associated with, such as improved test scores or less school disruptions? Put another way, is educating for character a worthwhile end in itself or just a means to some other goal?

By now you know my answer: Character education, understood as an essential end in itself—is, in my mind, THE most important goal of schooling—and for that matter, parenting as well. It also happens to be the best available means to other important educational goals such as academic learning. As I said, "good character education is good education."

Long ago, my colleague Larry Nucci cautioned me to avoid making the argument that character education increases academic achievement. If we implement character education *in order to* raise test scores (or other indices of academic success), then character education is not an authentic priority. Rather it is only a means to an end and not an end in itself. To reduce character education to being just a means to academic success minimizes the importance of nurturing human goodness. More-over, if for some reason the academic payoff from character education doesn't happen as soon or as significantly as some hoped, and that is our main rationale for doing it, some people may start to feel that all this work to develop good character is not worth the effort. So, we must value nurturing goodness simply because goodness matters.

The second test of the authenticity of a school's prioritization of character educa-tion is to ask whether we say that "character education is our highest priority" but then do not practice what we preach. This brings us back to Argyris and Schoen's dis-tinction between "espoused theory" and "theory in action." As we shall see shortly in our discussion of effective practices of prioritization, one first step to show the prior-itization of character education is in fact rhetorical, professing it to be a priority and talking about it. Many schools and school leaders *claim* to value character education. For some of them, their actions back up their words. However, for others, their words are hollow. They may or may not know it, but nonetheless, their words belie their true priorities. In other words, in those cases their prioritization of character education is inauthentic.

Not only should character education be an authentic priority, but also it must be *the* priority if schools are to succeed in the broader mission of both teaching academics and preparing future responsible citizens, particularly in nurturing the flourishing of human goodness.

There are five kinds of Prioritization practices, each of which will be treated sepa-rately in their own chapters: (1) rhetoric, (2) resource allocation, (3) school climate/culture, (4) structures, and (5) leadership. Each kind of practice is also listed in the worksheet at the end of Part II on Prioritization, so you can see how you are doing on the various practices, identify what you want to work on, discuss that with colleagues, plan action steps, and so on.

6

●●●●●

Making Character Education a Priority: Rhetorical Prioritization

One common and important way of prioritizing character education is how we talk about schools and kids. This set of practices, Rhetorical Prioritization, is not only about *how* we talk about character education. But even *if* we do, some schools eschew it and even think it should not be done. Some schools consider it or even do it but do not talk about it much or at all. Others talk about it all the time, although they may or not do it, or do it effectively. Rhetorical Prioritization is concerned only with what we say. What we do is covered by the other elements of Prioritization (and all the other Design Principles of PRIMED).

"Talking about" (both in speech and in writing) is typically the first step that schools take in their journeys to implement character education. One pejorative phrase used to ridicule character education is that it is merely "words on the wall." Many schools quickly purchase or produce character-focused posters and other graphic images and proudly display them in hallways, classrooms, and public areas like the cafeteria or gymnasium. They also put messages about character and character education on marquees in front of the school, on stationery, and on their electronic "faces" such as their web pages. There is nothing wrong with publicizing character strengths, virtues, values, and character education in this way. In fact, this is an evidence-based practice, or we would not be including it here.

However, I suggest you think of such rhetorical emphasis as a highlighter pen. Such pens highlight something of value, something substantial, something that already exists. If one were to highlight a blank page, it would be pointless. Likewise, character education rhetoric should bring salience to the commitment to and implementation of character education in the school. If there is no implementation that goes beyond simply promoting the importance of character, then rhetorical emphasis is as pointless as highlighting a blank page. Therefore, Rhetorical Prioritization as a first step might actually be pointless.

In fact, it can be harmful, especially for adolescents. Adolescents need no help being skeptical, even cynical. Proclaiming that the school is a "school of character" or that we value "respect, responsibility, and caring" when the school has a weak (or even average) culture in which bullying, disrespect, and a general lack of concern for the welfare of others are present, even common, breeds cynicism. Kids, especially adolescents, are Geiger counters for hypocrisy. They do not miss it. In fact, they are looking for adults to stumble and to appear less mature and good than the kids think they themselves are. It is part of the journey and work of adolescence to psychologically establish oneself as mature and equal to, even superior to, adults. Want to make a TV show popular with adolescents or even younger kids? Just make the kid characters smarter than the adult character. It will be a smash hit. It always has been a recipe for such success.

In many ways, using rhetoric to proclaim character education as a priority is the espoused theory we talked about earlier. It is what we profess, whether or not we do it. This can take more than one form. If we profess something with our lips but do not sincerely mean it in our hearts, then we are guilty of being intentional hypocrites. But quite often, the gap between what we espouse and what we do is not because we are being intentionally deceptive. Rather it is because we do not see the gap between what we claim (espoused theory) and what we actually do (theory in action). We *think* we are prioritizing character education in what we really do but are blind to the fact that we really are not. This is much more common than you might think.

Once you have a "theory in action" with implementation steps underway, such as building a positive school culture, then it is time for the highlighter pen of Rhetorical Prioritization. When Wolfgang Althof established a series of character education schools in Switzerland, he urged schools to wait until they had fully developed their initiatives before they wrote their mission statements. His reasoning was that "it is much easier to find the right words if you just have to write up what already is an informed consensus." So how can you do that? This one is quite simple, much more so than most of the rest of the strategies and Design Principles we will cover. The fact that it is relatively easy to implement is one reason it is so common, both in strong character education schools as well as in schools that are doing little to nurture the flourishing of human goodness.

Perhaps the most common first prioritization step is to agree upon, name, and make as prominent as possible a set of "core values," "character strengths," or "virtues" (terms used interchangeably in this book, with apologies to my philosopher colleagues). These are your "words on the wall." They give you a common language, which is a significant and useful achievement. Character.org dedicates much of the first three principles of their *11 Principles Framework for Schools* to what it calls core values. Its very first principle defines good character as "understanding, caring about and acting upon *core ethical and performance values.*" Once your school or district gets into the project of choosing your target core values, important questions and decisions will confront you. Among them:

- Where should the core values come from?
- Who should be involved in selecting them, or at least having input into their selection?
- How many core values should we adopt?
- What do we do with them once we have them?
- Should this be our first step?

Let us take each in turn.

Where should the concepts come from?

There are many choices, including not having any core values/strengths/virtues. Remember, character education is a *way of being* more than a way of talking. Therefore, you could just decide to *be* character and not create a list of concepts. However, it is often very helpful to have such a set of character concepts as organizing concepts and guideposts. They essentially can come from three places. (1) they can be passed down through the history of the school (or school district); (2) they can be selected by a person or group; (3) they can be adopted from an existing framework or model, such as the Character Counts *Six Pillars of Character* or the 24 character strengths of Positive Psychology, among many others.

Table 6.1 11 Principles Framework for Schools: A Guide to Cultivating a Culture of Character

Principle 1	**Core Values** are defined, implemented, and embedded into the school culture
Principle 2	The school **defines "character" comprehensively** to include thinking, feeling, and doing
Principle 3	The school uses a **comprehensive, intentional, and proactive approach** to develop character
Principle 4	The school creates a **caring community**
Principle 5	The school provides students with **opportunities for moral action**
Principle 6	The school offers a **meaningful and challenging academic curriculum** that respects all learners, develops their character, and helps them succeed
Principle 7	The school fosters students' **self-motivation**
Principle 8	All **staff share the responsibility** for developing, implementing, and modeling character
Principle 9	The school's character initiative has **shared leadership and long-range support** for continuous improvement
Principle 10	The school engages **families and communities as partners** in the character initiative
Principle 11	The school **assesses** its implementation of character education, its culture and climate, and the character growth of students on a regular basis

Source: Used with permission of Character.org

To decide among these options, let us examine three critical considerations: Ownership, philosophical legitimacy, and the generational nature of schools.

People tend to take better care of things for which they feel some sense of ownership. After all, when was the last time you changed the oil in a rental car or moved the furniture and vacuumed in a hotel room? Having stakeholders create their own set of values increases their sense of ownership in the concepts and in the character education initiative. It is also an example of Empowerment, the fifth Design Principle.

There are great models out there with vetted lists of values (note I am using the word values to represent values, virtues, character strengths, or whatever one wants to call a set of core character concepts). They are well worth considering. What I recommend, however, is to have a process for examining and affirming the model's given list, rather than taking them without reflection. This can give some sense of ownership. It is even worthwhile to adapt them to local considerations. Perhaps you will add some concepts to the adopted list. Or delete one or two that do not seem to be as compelling to the school stakeholders involved in the vetting process. Or use synonyms for some or all of them that might seem more comfortable for your population. Most such lists however come with curricula, lessons, etc. Removing concepts may cause confusion. It is the process of examining how these words tie into the personal stories of the stakeholder and affirming them that is most important here for stakeholder buy-in. Helping stakeholders name their personal core values not only helps establish authentic school values, it lays the groundwork for a strong school culture. Moreover, you do not have to use the curricula to adopt the words.

It is also important, wherever the concepts come from, to be sure they pass philosophical/ethical muster. Are they truly justifiable goods? Should we want to possess and develop them? Having a public process to be sure of that, even asking a philosopher to help, is a good idea.

Many years ago, Amitai Etzioni, the founder of the Communitarian movement, invited me to collaborate on a paper on character education. He argued that core values should be a local community decision. After all, that is the heart of communitarianism. I countered that not all communities are wise or even moral. Would we want some of the more reprehensible communities to be justified in picking racist, xenophobic, sexist, etc. concepts? There are bigoted communities all around the world. He heard the argument and even agreed to let me include language on universal morality. Sadly, his commitment to his Communitarian vision eventually overrode this, and he buried the paper and replaced it with a more consistently Communitarian perspective that did not include the possibility of universal or philosophical criteria for selected values.

I faced the same issue when I lived in Wisconsin. The State Department of Education published a position paper that said two incompatible things: (1) they believe in universal values and (2) each community should choose their own set of universal values. I was stunned at the paradox here. At the same time in Wisconsin, there was a lot of press about a white supremacist group that had carved out their own town and declared themselves independent of the US. They were teaching their children violence, racism, and hatred. Would we want them to "choose their own values," and, perhaps more importantly, should we then treat them as morally equal to all others simply because they were "communally" chosen?

It is important to note that when schools, communities, and/or school districts actually choose a set of values, they are almost always very legitimate and ethical ones. I have found that the five that are usually part of any list are some versions of respect, responsibility, fairness, honesty, and compassion. These also are the words at the core of the Six Pillars of Character from Character Counts and the core concepts from the Institute for Global Ethics, both of which used broad constituencies to identify what they consider a universal set of values.

We want the members of the school community to connect to the values and ideally a sense of shared ownership for them. And that they are justifiable values. However, even if we accomplish that, we need to understand that schools are generational organizations. By that I mean that the population grows up and moves out. This is clearest with the kids. In a K-5 elementary school, every six years there is a completely new population from six years earlier. Every three years in a typical middle school. Every four years in a typical high school.

It is not just the kids; there is less regular turnover in staff as well. School leaders often struggle with their school having a set of words but no idea of their origin. It is a wise idea to build into the historical rhythms of the school a regular review of those values. At least every six years in the K-5 schools, three years in the middle school, four years in the high school, etc. you should have a process for revisiting the values. Perhaps it is a "press re-start" process. Maybe it is just a community "re-considering" process. Even if it leads to a decision to keep them as they are (which is the most common outcome), it gives voice and ownership to those who now comprise the school community. Giving new teachers and students the opportunity to name and share their own core values and reflect on how they fit the school values alone would be beneficial.

Who should be involved in selecting them?

As Character.org's First Principle suggests, this should be a communal process. I prefer that all school stakeholders, including students, have a say—or at least that all stakeholder groups have adequate representation in the process. When Avis Glaze was Superintendent of a district in Ontario Canada, she decided to use a communal process to select a set of core values. She invited members not only of the traditional school stakeholder groups (administrators, parents, and teachers) but also members of the broader community, such as media, clergy, government, and law enforcement. Over three evenings about 200 people grappled with personal differences and semantic nuances and ultimately hashed out their shared set of selected core values for their community and the schools within it.

There are many excellent resources to help guide such a process. CharacterPlus has a long-standing, evidence-based, and widely used process detailed in their *CharacterPlus Way*. Charles Elbot and David Fulton describe a very systematic process in their book *Building an Intentional School Culture*. Moreover, Character.org gives many examples in their Principle 1 of the *11 Principles Framework for Schools*, as does Tom Lickona in his set of books on character education.

How many concepts should we adopt?

There is no definitive answer for this. I have seen everything from no concepts to a single concept all the way up to 40 for a "word of the week" structure. Caring School Community does not have a set of values. Bristol Elementary in Webster Groves (MO) used to have one value: Peace. Tom Lickona's Center for the fourth and fifth Rs was based on two: Respect and responsibility. Phil Vincent proposed expanding that to three by adding caring. I know many schools with a set of four. Character Counts has Six Pillars of Character. The Jubilee Centre lists eight Knightly Virtues. Many schools have nine so they can focus on one per month of the school year. The Virtues Project lists 100.

I prefer fewer values so they can be dealt with more clearly and in greater depth. And so that people can actually readily remember them all and invoke them as needed. Sometimes it helps to align the number with some characteristic of the school, for instance grade levels. If a middle school has three core values, then they can spend a full year on each, for example. I also think, however, that one should have an eye toward developmental (age) considerations as well. Five-, six-, and seven-year-olds can be overwhelmed by too many concepts, so simpler and shorter may be better.

By the way, the same goes for school or classroom rules. I knew one school that had a single rule: Always be in the right place at the right time doing the right thing. That was it. Kathryn Wentzel's research on middle schools suggests that having fewer rules corresponds to better learning and better character. That is something to think about and that would make a great topic for staff discussion. How many values is the right number for our school? Why do classrooms with fewer rules have better academic achievement and student behavior? What should we do about it?

What do we do with them once we have them?

Well, a lot. Here is a set of steps of increasing complexity that one can take in embedding the values after their selection.

First, define them. Ideally, like selecting the values in the first place, defining them should be a communal process. An interesting way of doing this was from an elementary school in New Jersey that used a variation of a 360-degree evaluation. Students, parents, and teachers separately created three sets of definitions of their six core values. Then they created a trifold character report card, with one page listing the student definitions, one listing the teacher definitions, and one listing the parent definitions. Teachers evaluated the students using the teacher definitions. Parents evaluated their own child using the parent definitions. Moreover, students evaluated themselves using the student definitions. However they are defined, the definitions should be clear, accurate, and kid-friendly.

Once you define them, they should be made widely known. Certainly, this includes publicizing them through rhetorical prioritization, but it also includes studying them. Which should lead to applying them conceptually; for example, by analyzing literature, art, history, sport, etc. to see where and how the values are manifested.

After defining them, it may be helpful to anchor them behaviorally. In other words, to agree what each one looks like in actual behavior. What does respect look like? What does caring or fairness look like? This can be general or can be differentiated in a variety of ways. For example, what does respect look like from student to teacher, student-to-student, teacher-to-student, and so on? What does respect look like in the hallway, in the classroom, in the bathroom, in the cafeteria, on the ball field? Then do the same for the lack of the value, that is, what does disrespect look like? Of course, making this a communal process, whether at the district, school, or classroom level, is optimal.

Just as I would suggest for classroom (or school) rules, it is best, however, to skew toward the positive and away from the negative. Then, after defining and behaviorally anchoring them, it is a good idea to create a rubric. The first such rubric I encountered came from Columbine Elementary School in Colorado, an early National School of Character (Note: The Columbine is the Colorado state flower, so it is not surprising that the name is prevalent). In their case, the teachers created a rubric of levels of each of their six core character concepts. In other schools, more of the stakeholder community is involved in creating such a rubric, including the students. Students then study the rubric and learn the levels of each concept. What is ideal honesty and how can one fall short of it? This is a powerful way of both learning the concepts more deeply and having a meaningful set of concepts for dealing with undesirable behaviors. When a student acts less than fully respectfully or responsibly, then the conversation about the behavior in question can focus on measuring it against the rubric. Where were you on the rubric? What would you have needed to do to be more respectful/responsible? Having learned the rubric, they can usually evaluate and critically analyze their own behavior and suggest better alternative behaviors. This can be immensely helpful in developmental discipline (or any enlightened and productive discipline), something we will deal with later. Its power is evidenced in part by the discovery at Columbine that the students were exporting the rubric to their homes, and parents were learning it.

Ultimately, making these concepts come alive in the heads, hearts, and hands of students and all other school stakeholders is the goal. It is not enough to simply "know" them (the "head" of character) by studying and displaying and analyzing them. Much of this book, especially the section on Intrinsic Motivation, will examine ways to do this.

Should this be our first step?

This is an interesting and tough question and one that is not asked frequently enough. You might assume you start there; after all, it is the first of the 11 Principles Framework for Schools. However, as chronicled in the Francis Howell Middle School character video, when Principal Amy Johnston started the character education journey, she assumed that core values would be the first step, but it really depends where your school is with regard to many factors. Significant push back from many FMHS staff (Whose values are these? Why are they our core values?) led to a yearlong staff discussion of their own values and what it means to be a character educator. As Amy tells it, she (wisely) put the question of which values aside while allowing the staff to grapple with the daunting proposition of teaching character. They (wisely too) realized that in order to *teach* character, they would have to *be* character, and that understandably frightened many of them. They shelved the initial emphasis on picking values to grappling with the daunting task of teaching character and *being* character and later returned to the core values, using a community-wide process that took almost a year to settle on four core values.

Even though Amy now has earned her doctorate in character and citizenship education and is a national and international Eleven Principles trainer and evaluator for Character.org, she advises principals to work on themselves and their staff culture before starting the process of selecting core values, just as they did at Francis Howell Middle School.

I suggest opening up the question of how to sequence the steps for your particular circumstances. I do, however, have a simple generic strategy. Year One: Professional development for the Principal (more on this in Chapter 10). Year Two: Principal leading staff in grappling with the entire prospect of character education and beginning professional development for them. Year Three: Now you are ready to start implementing for the students. I realize that waiting two years to do any character education for the students is a bit of a challenging delay of gratification for most educators. I do not mean this categorically and literally, however; rather, it is more a matter of emphasis. First the administration, then the teachers, then the kids.

●●●●●

More Rhetorical Strategies

It should be clear that it is important to talk about character and to have useful language with which to do so. Core character concepts are certainly a main part of that. However, so are other forms of shared language. Both Tom Lickona and Charles Elbot/ David Fulton offer examples of mottos, mission statements, touchstones, and other, as Phil Vincent calls them, "sacred documents of character education." All of these can be ways to place rhetorical priority on character education.

Mission statements are a good example. As part of our year-long Leadership Academy in Character Education (LACE), all participating school leaders are required to do a series of "homework" assignments (actually they are not to be done at home but rather at school with a representative character education team, a form of collaborative leadership). One of them is to report their sacred documents (mission statement, vision statement, touchstone or motto, value statements) and then critically examine them to see if they adequately prioritize character development and education. A mission statement should be a purpose statement, an articulation of why the school even exists. What is the purpose of the school? As such, it should talk about the priorities of the school and should be used to drive policy and practice. Sadly, that appears to be rare.

Mission statements are required (at least in US schools) and hence are sadly consequently treated more as a "check off" item on a "must do" list than as an important activity and resource for the health and success of the school. Having a mission statement should be a guiding light, a compass, for keeping an institution on course toward its primary objectives, helping to Prioritize them. Hal Urban, in his book *Lessons from the Classroom* which reflects on his 35 years as a high school teacher doing exemplary character education, goes so far as to show how he created and shared a "teacher mission statement" and asked his students to let him know if he slipped in practicing it. Then he asked his students to create a class mission statement.

Schools would do well to take these statements more seriously as statements of their prioritization. This is why I ask the participants in our Leadership Academy in Character Education to constructively critique their own mission statements. I have found that this is actually very challenging for most educational leaders. They simply do not see the lack of clear emphasis on character development as a stated school purpose or priority. They see terms like "life-long learners" as suggesting character education is a priority, until I not so gently point out that effective criminals and terrorists are life-long learners. They just figure out better ways to avoid detection and adjust to law enforcement strategies and innovations.

Similarly, many mission statements focus only on performance character and not on moral character. I managed to create a tempest in a teapot and get myself to be persona non grata at a local school district, Parkway School District. It is important to note that Parkway is a truly exemplary district and now a National District of Character, led by an authentic and talented leadership team. I was waiting to meet the then new superintendent, Keith Marty, for the first time. Outside his office was the district mission statement, which, like most, did not mention moral character concepts. It focused on ensuring "all students are capable, curious and confident learners." In my typical "bull in a china shop" mode, the first thing I said to Keith when he came to greet me was that I did not like the mission statement. In the ensuing discussion, I told him that effective terrorists are "capable, curious and confident."

I did not know this was a new mission statement that came from a lengthy community-wide process. I quickly became a pariah in the district. Until I received an email from a school counselor who said, "Guess what Dr. B? Parkway no longer educates terrorists. We just voted to add caring to the mission statement." Now it reads, "The Mission of the Parkway Schools is to ensure all students are capable, curious, caring and confident learners who understand and respond to the challenges of an ever-changing world." Oh, and I am no longer a pariah at Parkway. . . . I think. Kudos to them for listening.

7

•••••

Prioritization Through Resource Allocation

It certainly is desirable for schools and school members to talk about character education as a priority. However, words are not enough and can often be hollow. There is a saying that if one wants to know someone's priorities, look at their calendar and credit card bills. Where do they put two of their most important resources, money and time? One way to see the authenticity of the rhetorical priority is to see how they allocate those and other resources. Are there funds available for character education? When students or staff request resources for a character education project, is it more or less likely to be granted compared to athletic or academic requests?

Pat McEvoy, now Principal of Bayless (MO) High School, once said, when he was principal at another high school, that the role of a principal was like that of a Hollywood movie producer. He did not mean that you drive a Ferrari and wear $1,000 sunglasses. The talent for movies mostly resides in the director, writers, actors, etc. The producer's job is to get them the resources they need to do their best work. That may be money, but it may also be talent, time, or locations and so on. Pat lives by these words. In his school, priority is given to finding the funding for student- and teacher-initiated character education initiatives. Pat said that if students or staff came to him with a request for funds for character education, it was not his job to second-guess the merits of the project but simply to find the funds for them. In his own words, "if I have to buy fewer footballs for the football team" then he would do that to fund character education.

Principals need to ask themselves where character education is (if anywhere) in the school budget. Is there a budget line for it? If there is, is it a reasonable amount? Is it a fundraising priority? What suggestions or guidelines do they give to the parent organization or the school district budget office for fiscal needs for character education, if any?

However, money is not the only resource needed for optimal character education. Beyond the credit card bills, we have to look at principals' calendars, most notably the school master schedule, because time is a precious commodity too. As Amy Johnston has said, "If we don't find time in our master schedules for building relationships, they won't happen."

We tend to find time for what we most value, so when educators say they do not have time for character education, they are deprioritizing it. Some exemplary character education principals have gotten creative in finding time for character education. Some secondary level principals have turned their homerooms/advisories either fully or in part into character building time. Those who did not have homerooms or advisories have found creative ways to shave time from regular classes (a few minutes each) and passing time (a minute from each class transition) to find 20 or 30 minutes every day. Others have looked at their early release days (half days of school) and noted that these are inefficient days for academic instruction as most classes are cut in half.

Consequently, they abandoned academic lessons those few days of the year and used them fully for character education.

Another interesting spin on school time is what I call "the sanctity of beginnings." Many take the first day, days, or even weeks of the year to be exclusively or mainly dedicated to character education, for example, focusing on building relationships, collaboratively establishing classroom and whole school norms, and developing an emotional bond to and comfort level with the school. Kristen Pelster had one goal for the first day of school. She wanted to structure the day so that every student would leave the school at the end of the day either thinking or saying, "This is the coolest school in the world! I can't wait to come back tomorrow." A brilliant goal. Amy Johnston dedicated the first week of school mainly to building relationships, community, and character. She assigned each academic department to do one lesson from Hal Urban's book *Lessons from the Classroom*, so students would not repeat lessons in different classes. Hal's book is largely about the first three weeks of the year in his high school classrooms. Two of his favored innovations were about a beginning—but not the beginning of the year—rather they were about the beginning of every class period . . . all year long. One was greeting each student at the door and the other was to start class with either good news, a compliment, or something humorous. The point here is that not all time is equally significant, but beginnings usually are (beginning of the school year, semester, week, day, class period, etc.).

It is not only beginnings that may need to be honored and/or re-dedicated. Eric Soskill, an elementary teacher now in Maryland, when teaching fifth grade in St. Louis, recognized that the last 15 minutes of the day were wasted time, because the kids were in "leaving mode" and "clock watching." He recouped that time by having his students ready to depart 15 minutes before dismissal, with the room cleaned up, backpacks packed, and coats on. Then the final 15 minutes of the day were a class meeting reflecting on the day and what they had learned. These may be the only kids on the planet who, when asked by their parents "what did you learn today at school?" not only did not answer "nothing" but also enthusiastically told what they had learned.

Over the past two decades, I have sadly watched the erosion of site-controlled professional development time, especially for character education, in schools. In our What Works in Character Education project, we identified 33 character education programs that research shows to be effective. Every single one included at least optional, often mandatory, professional development in character education, because effective character education does not come fully assembled in a box.

Professional development is a matter of time, but it is also often a matter of money. There may be a cost for the professional development, and there may be money needed for substitute/supply teachers to allow educators to participate. There are also choices as to the focus of professional development. Most typically, schools are more supportive of instructional/academic-focused professional development than character-focused professional development. This says a lot about what the true priorities are, no matter what the rhetorical prioritization may be.

8

School/Classroom Climate and Prioritization

Character education is about *being*. This applies not only to how individuals *be*, but also to how larger social entities *be*. It matters deeply how the classroom, the middle school academic team, the high school grade level, the entire school, and even the school district function. We will focus on the notion of individual Modeling later. Here we will deal with the larger sociological emphasis on school and/or classroom climate. If we create and support climates that align with character development, we are demonstrating Prioritization. In different guises and under different names, this has long been recognized. John Dewey's emphasis on democratic schooling, Philip Jackson's notion of the hidden curriculum, Lawrence Kohlberg's emphasis on moral atmosphere, etc. all are earlier versions of the focus of today's school climate movement. If we want schools that optimally nurture the flourishing of human goodness, then we have to see an emphasis on building a positive school climate. In reviewing research, we found five ways that prioritizing school climate supports character development.

- School-wide focus on character education.
- Trust among teachers.
- Perception of safety.
- Promotion of caring schools and classrooms.
- Assessing school climate.

School-wide Focus on Character Education

Hal Urban reports that in his over 30 years as a high school teacher, he was largely a lone character education wolf. He did brilliant work in his classroom (see *Lessons from the Classroom*), but it never spread beyond his classroom door. He recounts the story of a foreign exchange student, who was so impressed with both the classroom culture and the behavior of the students in Hal's classes, in contrast with other classes he took from other teachers, that he suggested that Hal call a meeting of all the high school faculty. The purpose would be to teach them his classroom climate practices, many of which we will recount as examples of PRIMED. Hal wisely realized that would not go over very well with his colleagues, many of whom were already disparaging of character education.

One of the common laments from both school leaders and teachers is that they cannot get sufficient buy-in from staff. They detect apathy about character education, even some antipathy. Part of Prioritization, particularly a school-wide focus, is increasing the buy-in of all stakeholders. We frequently ask school leaders to create a plan for increasing the buy-in of all stakeholder groups. We define buy-in as both more members of each group buying in and deeper involvement by them as well. School leaders often struggle with understanding how to do this effectively.

There are three effective principles of increasing stakeholder buy-in, and they tend to overlap with other elements of PRIMED. First, build positive relationships with and among them (more on this in the section on Relationships). Second, authentically empower them to be co-owners and co-authors of the character education initiative (more on this in the section on Empowerment). Third, equip them with the competency to participate in character education. This refers to the investment in professional development that we discussed already, but it also has to do with what Julie Frugo, Head of School of Premier Charter School in St. Louis, calls being a Professional Growth Leader (more on this shortly). Such leaders create a school-wide climate of nurturing the professional growth of all members of the school staff. When people feel efficacious toward engaging in character education, they will buy in more deeply.

However, being school-wide does not mean only having everyone on board. It also means implementing in ways that impact the entire school. Sometimes we simply forget to include certain key stakeholder groups such as secretaries, custodians, cooks, and bus drivers. I am always impressed when I am asked to provide professional development and all members of the staff are present, and even more so when they are part of a team that travels outside the school in order to attend professional development or conferences. Two special education high schools in St. Louis (Neuwoehner and Northview) routinely send all of their paraprofessionals to earn character education certification from CharacterPlus.

Additionally, some programs are targeted toward only subsets of the school, whether groups of people, structural elements of the school (e.g., only athletes or top scholars or special education students), or other subdivisions. There are, for example, many leadership programs or peer conflict resolution programs that impact only a minority of the students. All students need to learn the skills and values of leadership. Moreover, all students need to learn about, practice, and engage in peer conflict resolution. These are life skills that all need . . . including the adults.

Rather than having a principal's advisory team consisting of a few star students, have a weekly principal's advisory forum in which different students participate each week, and all students eventually get a chance. One elementary school in Belleville, Illinois, instead of creating school committees of students, simply listed the committees on large sheets of paper posted in the gymnasium. Any student who wanted could sign up for whichever they found attractive. One might be a recycling team. Another would set up and break down rooms for large meetings (moving chairs and tables, etc.). Another might be ambassadors for visitors, transfer students, and other guests. Then the staff would simply call on as many from the list as they needed for each event. While not all are involved, all have the opportunity.

Some character education programs explicitly include school-wide elements. Caring School Communities includes a school-wide emphasis on creating and revising school-wide traditions and events to foster character development. For example, rethink the typical science fair from a competitive event that fosters cheating and ill will to one that is a shared learning exposition where all students learn from each other rather than compete with each other for a prize.

When Mark Eichenlaub was principal of Jefferson Elementary in the Belleville 118 (IL) school district, he instituted a beginning of the day, whole school event. All students came to the gymnasium before going to their classes, and there was a whole school meeting to set the proper tone for the day, celebrate and learn about character, and generally build a positive identity within a great school. Rob Lescher, principal of Busch Middle School in the St. Louis Public Schools, starts every day with silent reading by all school members, including staff and administration. All come to the gymnasium as the first stop in the day, sit quietly, and read to start the day right and to create a positive climate for learning and cooperation and respect.

However one does it, thinking from the perspective of the whole school is an important and effective ingredient in creating a school climate that optimally nurtures the flourishing of goodness in students. This expands "no child left behind" to "no one left behind."

● ● ● ● ●

Trust in Teachers

Without interpersonal trust, it is difficult to have a positive climate in any organization. The most cogent statements on this in the field of character education come from Marilyn Watson, Anthony Bryk, and Megan Tschannen-Moran

Watson, the author of *Learning to Trust*, has provided a strong conceptual framework for understanding the nature and source of interpersonal trust and then a practical model of how to nurture and sustain trust in the classroom, both among students and between teacher and students. She uses this as a platform for her model of Developmental Discipline, which we will discuss in the section on Developmental Pedagogy. The key for us here is that building trust needs to be intentional, strategic, and fully inclusive. You cannot simply count on being kind-hearted and good-willed. I often say that most teachers come to teaching because they have golden hearts for kids. They also often assume that their golden hearts will be enough to generate positive classroom climates, healthy relationships, and trust. And they will. Except for the kids that need it most. That is why it must be strategic, intentional, and inclusive. That is the real meaning of "no child left behind." If students do not trust their teachers and do not feel safe with them, it will be impossible to nurture character development or academic success and create the type of climate that supports such development.

Bryk and Schneider's study in the Chicago Public Schools found that the level of "relational trust" among teachers in the schools was directly related to the academic success of their schools. More trust among the staff, more academic success. Tschannen-Moran has elegantly deconstructed the nature and formation of trust of the leader in her book *Trust Matters*.

● ● ● ● ●

Sense of Safety

The Collaborative for Academic, Social and Emotional Learning (CASEL.org) concluded in their research reviews that an important element in effective practice is that schools are physically and psychologically safe places to be. As noted earlier, we expand that to include racially/culturally and intellectually safe. It is also important that the members of the school community perceive the school that way. Just because adults think the school is safe does not mean that students or other stakeholders do. Moreover, because most perceive it as such does not mean all do. A child—or an adult—who has been targeted by a bully will not feel that way. A child or adult who has been systematically excluded from social groups or activities will not feel that way.

When Jack Benninga and I studied elementary schools in California, we found school safety to be one of the elements of character education that most strongly predicted the academic success of schools. Kids learn best when they feel safe. I remember when my son, then in college, did me a favor and delivered something to an urban high school. He came back stunned at the prison-like atmosphere of the high school. Metal detectors. Armed guards. Etc. That school climate made him feel unsafe.

Perceived safety is not merely the absence of overt threats. That is a low bar. A higher bar is the development of a welcoming, inclusive community. Many educators ask me how they can effectively educate for character development when they have high mobility rates with half of their students not beginning and/or ending the school year in the same school. My answer is that every challenge is an opportunity in disguise. I encourage them to think of the mobility as an opportunity to intentionally nurture a welcoming community. All schools have some mobility (transfer students, long-term replacement teachers, etc.). All schools have generational churn. The oldest students graduate and move on and a new group of youngest students enters each year. Teachers and other staff retire and are replaced. Hence, you should have structures in place to welcome and say goodbye to those folks. This makes the school intentionally welcoming. Moreover, schools with high mobility rates have the opportunity to be frequently welcoming.

Many schools have "ambassadors" who welcome visitors and give tours. Some have prepared Welcome Baskets, ready for new students and new families. These are typically created and assembled by students and often delivered by them as well.

In my Leadership Academy, I ask all participants to survey their staff about new teacher orientation and welcoming. Often it is nice but too limited and ineffective. New teachers need a minimum of two years to get through the initial shock of being a classroom teacher. Having an initial orientation and an assigned mentor may not be enough. Ask yourselves how effective your school's welcome and orientation are. More importantly, ask those hired the last few years. I recommend, where possible, ongoing weekly or monthly meeting of all new staff for a minimum of a year but ideally for two years.

Julie Frugo, Head of School of Premier Charter School, did her doctoral study on what she calls "The Professional Growth Leader", which is a leader who focuses on nurturing the professional growth of all whom she leads. She lives it in part by developing and leading a three-year coaching/orientation program for new teachers. She describes the pre-term orientation in the first year as follows:

> We bring them in for some development before the rest of the team is back, ranging 3 to 5 days. We work on getting to know the new teachers and hearing from them their wonders and worries about transitioning into their roles at PCS.

This culminates with:

> A newbie induction ceremony. We plan a happy hour type reception and the leadership, coaches and new teachers (and their guests) socialize and then it ends with the ceremony . . . the new teachers get a chance to hear from one of the leadership staff why specifically we hired them . . . we talk about what they said in their interview, what they did in the lesson they taught that we observed, etc. and they also get to hear why we think they are a perfect fit for our students. We thank their significant other, friend or guest for

supporting them as a teacher. We remind them about how teaching is hard and how they will need support and to remember how important self-care is and that is why their guests are so important to being there. Then they receive their badge/key and they are "official."

The rest of the first year has three components:

We plan activities to bond the group together, one of them being the challenge of coming up with a creative way to introduce themselves to the rest of the "family". . . . I'm always amazed at how this activity brings this cohort together and the excitement and applause that comes from the rest of the team. The time together before the rest of the 150 employees come back alleviates some of the anxiousness and shows the new teachers how important it is and how intentional we are when it comes to building a positive adult culture.

The next component is the monthly support seminar. This is . . . a 2.5 hour class each month where they learn and explore concepts related to building relationships and building a positive classroom culture. I lead the class with help from the coaches, but it is critical that they are connecting with me as the Head of School/Superintendent . . . and that there is an expectation to make this the top priority. They quickly learn that there is a chronological order to things, first you build the relationships and community in the classrooms, then the academic learning takes off. The activities and resources focus on understanding students from a developmental lens. We explore everything from trauma and realizing the biases we bring to the classroom to learning deeply about strategies like class meetings. We do things that may seem over the top. We provide a home cooked meal each time. It makes them feel cared for in a really special way. We provide them resources to use . . . books, sensory fidgets, etc. Everything we do is done with intentionality-we want to model how we want them to be with their kids.

The final component to the program is . . . coaching. . . . The coaches work individually with the teachers to set up observations, meetings/online discussions or a chance for the coach to go in and model a class meeting or a lesson. What happens each month is usually tied to the goals we are working on from the seminar, but it can also be tweaked based on the teacher's need. Sometimes coaches will go in and cover a class so the new teacher can go observe a peer, or they will videotape it . . . and watch it together.

We have an end of year coaching celebration. . . . The leadership, coaches and guests are invited and we celebrate and reflect. We share stories about their growth and we bust out artifacts that we have collected throughout the year as well as ask them to share from their reflection journals . . . they always get emotional . . . until we remind them that there is a year two.

The second year is referred to as a "grub and grow" year. The format is a monthly happy hour book study. . . . The content comes out of what was discovered in the first year as areas for further growth such as a deeper dive on Empowerment or Intrinsic motivation. Teachers are paired and choose the restaurant. There is plenty of "pre-work" in the form of videos and readings and reflection questions.

The third year is called the "share the wealth" year. Based on teacher surveys and reflections, each person crafts individual goals for year three. While there remain some whole-cohort meetings, much of the work becomes individual coaching around the individual's professional goals. This includes a "plunge experience" where the individual selects an activity that is a deep dive into an experience central to her goal. In the second half of the year, they run a conference for all the staff, and they create and present workshops around their personal explorations/goals. Coaches help them prepare and are the audience for a "dress rehearsal." Big celebratory end of the year.

As Julie (personal communication) notes,

Always end with a class/cohort circle meeting! Feedback we have gotten over the years has been so positive- some years cohorts have become so tight they go on to create book studying together and have even requested we get together for more master classes as they valued the meetings and discussions so much!

●●●●●

Caring Schools and Classrooms

Having a safe school is essential for effective character education but far from enough to define an ideal school climate. There is a long-standing theory in psychology called *self-actualization*. A self-actualized person is one who has reached the peak of a long process of development and maturation. As a motive, it is understood as a drive to fulfill one's greatest potential. Such people have a wide array of mature and desirable characteristics, such as accurate understanding of the world, trusting their own judgment, positive interpersonal relationships, compassion, and comfort with themselves. However, it is also understood that being self-actualized is only possible when a set of basic human needs are met. These conditions include basic physical needs like food, water, and shelter, but they also include safety. Before one can have a sense of belongingness (one of the three fundamental needs in Self-determination Theory), one must feel safe.

Hence, once one creates a sense of physical and psychological safety in schools, then one can layer on a sense of caring—or what Abraham Maslow—one of the main self-actualization theorists, calls "love and belonging."

The word *caring* may appear in more places in character education than perhaps any other character word. It is found in the names of school programs (such as Caring School Communities). It or a synonym (compassion, concern for others, love, etc.) is in almost every school list of core virtues or values. And so on.

There is an old expression in education for teachers: "Kids don't care how much you know until they know how much you care." The emphasis is on kids "knowing" you care. As we have noted for other issues like safety, it does not matter how much you care if kids do not know it. Any good con man can trap you if they can get you to believe they really care about you. It is the kid's perception that matters most here. We need to ensure both that schools and classrooms have caring climates and that students perceive it as such. Shortly we will address how important it is to assess systematically and effectively how students are experiencing the climate.

We can enhance the climate of caring by taking the time to get to know each other, which we will address in the section on Relationships. We can also create more caring climates by differentiating our instruction, classroom management, and communication to the unique needs of each student. Much of the issues of both safety and caring are being addressed currently by the movement toward Trauma-informed Care and Restorative Practices, which is addressed in the section on Developmental Pedagogy. Understanding what some kids might find threatening or uncaring because of their unique life experiences or the subcultures from which they come opens more possibilities for them to be and feel cared about.

Just greeting all kids and addressing them by name and knowing something personal about them, can contribute mightily to creating a caring environment. We will provide examples of this in the chapter on Relationships in school.

In the United States, where students move from one classroom to the next, some schools require staff to stand in the hallways at passing time, not to monitor student behavior but rather to engage in friendly conversation with students as they move throughout the school. Others strategically place adults around the school at the opening of school to ensure that each child is greeted at least five times before they begin the school day. Think about the difference in how children experience the school simply by how they perceive the motives of—and likely treatment by—the adults in the hallway, as prison wardens or as friendly greeters.

We will talk more about behavior management in the sections on Intrinsic Motivation and Developmental Pedagogy, but it is worth noting that flexible, collaborative, and restorative practices also can send the message of a caring environment. This is especially powerful as it happens in crisis, that is, when the child is being confronted about having violated some norm or rule or having hurt somebody physically or emotionally. We all know how emotionally devastating such moments can be. As Marilyn Watson challenges us, we need to re-construe such moments as opportunities for growth, both of the child and of the relationship, rather than simply moments to change behavior. Being treated humanely in crisis is another way of experiencing a school as a caring place.

●●●●●

Assessing School Climate

Character.org's 11th Principle is to assess one's character education initiative. This includes assessing school climate. The National School Climate Center's work centers on its policies for and methods of assessment of school climate. School climate is probably the most assessed variable in character education.

As part of our Leadership Academy, we require participants to design an assessment plan for their character education initiative. We ask them to consider three broad areas of assessment: Implementation; climate; student character development. Implementation and character development really challenge them, and they typically struggle mightily in understanding how to do both effectively. However, school climate is typically something they are already assessing, often very effectively.

Many schools and districts require annual climate surveys, often not only of students but also staff and even parents. Some measures exist that are scientifically validated and reliable. Some are free and some require purchase. Others simply create their own surveys about school climate. What is most important is just to do it and to do it on a regular basis.

Next most important is what you do with the data you collect. I always recommend that you treat character data the same way most schools now treat academic data; that is, you make the data public and engage in a professional process to scrutinize the data and decide what the data are telling you and how to move forward. Rick DuFour's *Professional Learning Community* model is one great framework for doing this. Have teachers reflect on the three PLC questions. (1) what do we want our students to know about character, our core values, etc.? (2) how will we know if they have learned it? (3) what will we do for students who have not? After all, we want the data we gather to drive school improvement.

9

•••••

Structural Prioritization

Another way of demonstrating the priority of character education is by creating structures that increase the presence of elements of character education. Often schools have sincere intentions to prioritize character education and may even engage in explicit rhetoric about those intentions, but the initiative sputters because there are no structures in place to make those intentions become a reality or to sustain them consistently.

Research has revealed five forms of structural strategies for prioritizing character education:

- Taking a comprehensive approach.
- Integrating it into all aspects of school life.
- Collaborating with other schools.
- Making it visible throughout and around the school.
- Assessing student character and giving feedback.

•••••

Taking a Comprehensive Approach

Character.org's second Principle of the *11 Principles Framework for Schools* promotes a comprehensive understanding of and approach to character education, and the third Principle addresses comprehensive implementation. This most centrally entails understanding the complexity of character. The Character.org definition of character focuses on three broad aspects of character: Cognition (knowledge, reasoning); affect (emotions, motivation); behavior (skills, actions). These are often remembered through the mnemonic device of head, heart, and hands.

The challenge of understanding character in this multifaceted way is the need to recognize that these different aspects of character develop in different ways. The "head" has multiple components, for which there may be different pedagogical methods. Learning what is right can be accomplished through traditional learning mechanisms like reading about character. Developing the competency to reason about social and moral issues, however, requires very different methods. This is a matter of critical thinking. To educate for critical thinking, in character or any academic subject, requires giving students the opportunity to grapple with concepts and issues, rather than giving them the answers to, in this case, moral questions. We have to build structures and policies for allowing students to explore social and moral issues and grapple both individually and collectively with what is actually right and wrong into our curricula and other aspects of school life such as behavior management. Telling may help them acquire knowledge, but it is not sufficient to help them develop the capacity to reason for themselves.

Moreover, the "heart" of character requires yet other strategies. This comes more from a sense of belonging to both the school and the adults that populate it and ensuring the school and the adults model the character about which we want students to care. We will explore this more deeply in the sections on Relationships, Intrinsic Motivation, and Modeling.

The "hands" of character require yet another pedagogical approach. Partly this is about giving students opportunities to practice and apply their character competencies, often through service to others. We will explore this in the section on Intrinsic Motivation. However, providing such opportunities is not enough. We have to help students acquire the skills they need to function as moral agents. We frequently ask educators to list the strategies they use in their schools for character development and then to identify which serve specific key elements of character education. "Skill-building" is one of those elements. It is one that is underrepresented in their character education approaches. We will address this more fully in the section on Developmental Pedagogy.

Kids do not come to school necessarily knowing how to disagree respectfully. Or how to resolve peer conflicts. Or how to manage their anger. Or to repair relationships, for instance when a friend is not speaking to them because they believe a lie they were told about them. We have to help them develop those skills. This is the central focus of social-emotional learning (www.casel.org). There are many excellent and evidence-based curricula for helping students acquire the interpersonal and intrapersonal skills of character. In many cases, we may know what is right (the head), authentically care about it (the heart), but fall short because we do not know how to do it (the hand).

Schools tend to miss this one more often than not. They tend to do one of two things about the hand of character. One, they assume that being in positions related to character (e.g., leadership roles, buddying or mentoring, etc.) will necessarily foster the acquisition of social-emotional competencies. Sometimes that works, but often it does not—or not fully enough. Two, they relegate skill teaching to the guidance curriculum, where the school guidance counselor periodically comes to the classroom to teach such skills. This is certainly a step in the right direction. However, it is preferable to have the classroom teachers do the teaching of character skills. Many classroom teachers respond to this suggestion by stating that they do not have time and/or skills to do that. The counter argument is that they cannot afford not to. Investing in the students' competencies to manage their own emotions and relate effectively to others, for example, at the beginning of the school year buys back a lot of time later and creates a positive school climate that supports optimal learning. Otherwise, the climate is less than optimal and the teacher will spend much time, all year, putting out social, emotional, and behavioral fires and struggling to motivate students, time away from quality instruction.

Having this differentiated approach to character education requires recognizing the complexity of character itself.

• • • • •

Integrating Character Education in All Aspects of School Life

Just like the notion that character is complex, and hence character education should be differentiated, it is important that we recognize that schools are very complex social institutions with lots of very variable parts. Consequently, we need to understand that we need to find ways to integrate character education into all aspects of school life. This is in fact the third principle of Character.org's 11 Principles Framework.

We want character education in our core academic lessons and in our guidance curriculum. Many schools also consider after-school activities as a place for character education. Perhaps most obvious is discipline. However, we also want to consider "specials" like art, music, and physical education; student leadership roles; and on the bus and in lunchroom norms and behavior. We have already discussed school-wide traditions like science fair, school Olympics, family ice cream socials, etc. And so on. In other words, it should be in *all* aspects of school life.

Once we realize that character education *should* be a priority in all aspects of school, we have to ensure that it actually happens . . . and happens effectively. Behavior management is a good example. This is a perfect place to nurture the flourishing of human goodness, but it is frequently done ineffectively and even counterproductively. The same can be said about most aspects of school life. Figuring out how to effectively integrate character education into the curriculum or how to engage in behavior management that is developmentally effective (more about both in the Developmental Pedagogy section) is critical to structural support for prioritizing character education.

● ● ● ● ●

Collaborating with Other Schools

In their review of Australian schools, Terry Lovat and his colleagues found that schools that were more successful at values education also were more likely to collaborate with other schools. Doing so is an indicator of the priority of character education in schools. This can be done within an organization (for example, within a school district) or more broadly.

One of my favorite examples is an elementary school in Georgia whose social studies curriculum included studying about voting and elections. And this included the notion and process of voter registration. The students became experts in voter registration. The elementary school took the students to the local high school and sent them into the lunchroom with registration forms. They approached the high school students, asked if they were old enough to vote and, if so, if they were registered. If they were not registered, the elementary "experts" offered to help them register.

Middle and high schools often partner with their feeder elementary schools and have their students volunteer to mentor and tutor their elementary partners.

A very smart thing any school can do to improve itself is simply to invest not in their own school but in the schools that send students to them ("feeder schools"). We frequently get reports from upper level schools that they can tell quickly which students come from which feeder schools by their behavior. Those coming from schools with serious, pervasive, and effective character education initiatives are the ones sending the "best" kids, kids who take learning seriously, are prosocial, and who add value to, rather than disrupting, the school climate and functioning. If a school can maximize such kids by investing in their feeder schools, why not do it? Have the upper school staff collaborate with the lower school staff, both about academics and character. Have the upper school staff simply show appreciation for the way the feeder school staff prepare students for the upper school. Collaborate on smoother vertical alignment and transitions. Everyone wins in such situations.

How a school thinks about such collaboration is also a measure of prioritization. I was working with the principals of the elementary school and middle school in a tiny rural district. They had four schools all on the same small campus (early childhood, elementary, middle, and high schools). I suggested to the middle school principal that his students should go to the elementary school to teach the younger kids about character. His response was hesitant. He justified it by saying the schools were not adjacent. In fact, they simply had to walk around the high school to access the elementary school, a matter of mere yards. A great opportunity that many schools would envy was wasted because character education was not a priority, turning a molehill into a perceived mountain.

When a police officer near Ferguson Missouri shot Michael Brown in August 2014, high school students in the region found that schools were not giving them the space and opportunity to talk about the incident and the issues undergirding it. Teachers did not feel competent to have such conversations, and some schools and districts forbade it. So CharacterPlus decided to be an intermural convener of many high schools for the purposes of meaningful conversation and social justice planning around issues such as race, segregation, class, belonging, social equity, justice, and student voice. They created Gateway2Change, an annual series of four meetings of students from a wide range of schools. The schools are grouped into clusters of four with the design of maximizing diversity and demographic representation. They even do "sibling" school shadowing where students spend time in each other's schools. Ultimately, the goal is to build school mechanisms, identify and nurture student leaders, and form school-based student teams to bring the work back to their school communities. This network brings priority to character education and was so successful it continues to this day.

●●●●●

Making Character Visible with Displays

A very common way of showing prioritization of character education is signage and displays. I will be brief here because this was discussed already under Rhetorical Prioritization.

Long ago, I was taken on a tour of two high schools that claimed to be "doing character education." One showed me only two things: A staff member and a mural. The staff member had an office off the gymnasium that was clearly meant as a storage closet. She was the character educator in the school, fully responsible for all that happened, which was very little. The mural was prominent and impressive. It depicted nine students, each holding a sign with one of their character words on it. I asked where the words came from and was told the school leadership chose them. I asked who the students in the mural were. I was told that they are the students who painted the mural. I concluded that character education here was under-resourced, and the mural was an example of self-promotion and mere repetition of adult-generated ideas.

The other high school simply had six signs prominently displayed, each with one of their character words. When I asked what they were doing with those character concepts, I was informed that they were not doing anything yet. They wanted to start with consciousness-raising. I imagined they were more likely to be doing cynicism raising.

Hal Urban cleverly used signage in his classroom. He had lessons attached to each sign (see *Lessons from the Classroom* for details). He would put up signs on a prearranged schedule, and then he would teach the lesson surrounding each sign as he put it up. He also created class norms and rules for many of them, to keep them salient and help students figure out how to *be* what the signs indicated.

Use signage to do two important things. First, to lend saliency to what is actually in the school or classroom. Signs do not create character, rather they help make it more salient and memorable. Second, as Urban did, use signs as visual indicators of important lessons that are directly linked to them. Signs do not teach, but they can be teaching aids.

●●●●●

Assessing Character and Giving Feedback

Earlier we talked about school climate and how part of an effective approach to school climate includes regularly and effectively assessing it. This is also a way to structurally prioritize character education. Another assessment example of structural prioritization is the assessment of student character development. I noted earlier that school leaders struggle with planning how to do this.

The most common ways schools assess student character are: (1) office referrals and other data on student misbehavior (such as suspensions and expulsions); (2) attendance; (3) academic achievement scores. While these are all indicators of the health and success of a school, they are imprecise indices of the specific impact of character education on student growth. The first is the one that comes closest, but it really is a measure of the Dark Side of character (misbehavior) and not the Force (human goodness). To make matters worse, the most helpful of those are office referrals, and most schools record them sporadically, unevenly, or not at all. Furthermore, there is often a lack of agreement among staff as to what, for example, respect is and how to respond to disrespect. Hence, those data are often pretty suspect. Suspensions and expulsions may be more rigidly controlled, but I hope they are also relatively rare.

Attendance, while partially an indicator of whether kids want to come to your school, is also affected by lots of other issues outside the control of the school and unrelated to the school's character education initiative. And while, as already noted, "Good character education is good education," and character education tends to raise academic test scores, such scores are not a measure of a student's character.

Nevertheless, it is a good idea to find a way to assess character. Sometimes, you have to get very creative. One principal cleverly would drop litter and money periodically and then watch to see what students did. But there are some standard psychological measures of character, such as the Mayerson Academy's VIA suite of measures and the Character Growth Index from the Mark Liston Group. Both of these are self-report measures of adolescent and/or adult character strengths.

As was pointed out already for the assessment of climate, it is important what you do with such data after you have collected it. Using a structured way of assessing character data, just as you do for academic data, is a good idea. Trying to "diagnose" individual kids is not, however, as most measures are not sensitive enough to make judgments about an individual's "goodness." Use the data for group analysis and to assess trends, such as answering, "Are we positively impacting the development of students' character?" CharacterPlus, in its *CharacterPlus Way*, includes a structure for processing character data.

Also, use such data for formative purposes. In other words, they can be given to students for them to self-assess and reflect on their own character, ideally to strategically plan for how to self-manage their own character journey to human goodness. We will talk about this further in the section on Developmental Pedagogy.

10

Leading Schools of Character

As the leader of a school, the principal (or head of school, or whatever term you use for the lead administrator of a school) has the greatest impact on the culture and climate of the school, on the optimal professional development and functioning of its staff, on its policies and practices, and ultimately on its priorities, functioning, and outcomes. So, for character education to be optimally effective and consequently for it to have the optimal impact on the flourishing of human goodness and academic success, the principal needs to be the organizational "champion" of the initiative. Ideally, the principal is not merely the "cheerleader" for character education but also has some expertise in the practice of character education. This suggests that the professional development of the principal should emphasize character education expertise, which is why I have invested so much time, energy, and resources in the Leadership Academy in Character Education (more on this later) for the past two decades. It is also why the Kern Family Foundation has recently begun to invest heavily in promoting character-focused leader professional development and education.

I have never seen a great school without a great leader, and I have never seen a great character education school without a great character educator as the leader. It is possible to delegate the expertise to others, and, in fact, it should be widely shared in concordance with the principles of Empowerment and investing in the adult culture, but ultimately the leader is the most influential person in this journey.

A critical concept here is authenticity (as it will be at other points in this book). I know many school leaders who think character education is a priority in their schools, but far fewer who think it is *the* priority in their schools, for whom it is a personal priority. If character development is not an authentic, personal priority for a principal, it cannot be a top priority for the school. One cannot ask others to commit to self-examination and modeling if you are not doing it yourself. If it is their personal priority, they will allocate resources accordingly. Remember Principal Pat McEvoy's metaphor earlier that principals are like Hollywood producers?

Jack Benninga, Director of the longest-standing character education center at Fresno State University, reminds us to also consider principal continuity. Indeed, keeping a good leader in place long enough to deeply and sustainably foster a healthy adult and whole-school culture—and a comprehensive approach to character education—is critical to effectiveness.

The Character of Leaders Who Lead for Character

There are many theories of and styles of leadership. Given our focus on PRIMED and its application to educating for character, we have narrowed the focus to three partially overlapping leadership frameworks: The Connected Leader, The Servant Leader and

Trustworthy leaders. These in turn generate a set of partially overlapping key characteristics of leaders. Most of these can be understood as the character strengths, personality characteristics, or even virtues of an ideal school (and character education) leader.

The Connected Leader

The Connected Leader is a model created by four of my former doctoral students, Julie Frugo, Amy Johnston, Brian McCauley, and Kevin Navarro. Julie is the head of school of Premier Character School in St. Louis, a National School of Character. Amy was the principal of Francis Howell Middle School in Missouri, another NSOC and now an international character education consultant. Brian and Kevin have both changed jobs after earning their doctorates with Brian—former Assistant Head of School for Admissions and Marketing at the Wasatch Academy in Utah—and Kevin, now the Head of School of Greensboro Montessori School in North Carolina. The Connected Leader (CL) has three main clusters: The Vulnerable Leader, the Transformational Leader, and the Professional Growth Leader and a measure of the best practices of all these leaders. This is a complex model, so we will only focus on some aspects of it here. The specific characteristics that will be discussed here are: Openness; humility; authenticity; ethical; inspirational; challenging; caring; empowering; and enriching.

Servant Leadership

Robert Greenleaf (www.greenleafcenter.org) described servant leadership as built on the premise that leaders should primarily serve those they lead. My good friend Dick Pieper, retired CEO of Pieper Power, an electrical contracting company, took that to heart when he started his corporate leadership journey. Being a Christian, he asked himself, "How would Jesus run a company?" His answer? By serving his employees and customers. And so he did, in part by continually surveying both groups about their needs, interests, and concerns and then trying to meet them. He consequently built a thriving national company, which, when he decided to retire, he chose to sell to his employees at a far lower price than other companies offered him, because he reasoned that they helped build its success. In many ways, this echoes Pat McEvoy's metaphor of school leader as Hollywood producer. My colleague, Melinda Bier, has, with the generous support of the John Templeton Foundation, studied the various renderings of servant leadership and narrowed down the core list of virtues of the servant leaders to the following set: Noble purpose; courage; humility; forgiveness; gratitude; foresight; empowerment; and stewardship. You can likely see the overlap between this list and the list derived from the Connected Leader model. Now we will take a closer look at the character of the leader for character. (Note that two great resources for many of these characteristics can be found at www.characterlab.org and www.greatergood.com).

Critical Characteristics of Great and Effective School Leaders

There are many perspectives on the nature of great leaders, and we cannot delve deeply into all of them. We will focus on those characteristics that have most to do with morality, ethics, and the development of a caring, ethical learning community among all school stakeholders. These are especially relevant to educating for character development. These characteristics are of most relevance in relating to adults, such as staff and parents, the central role of the leader. They are mainly from three frameworks: Connected Leader; virtues of servant leadership; characteristics of trustworthy leaders (identified by Megan Tschannen-Moran). There are 18 characteristics clustered into three areas: Inner strengths of the leader; characteristics that support the development of individuals and organizations; characteristics that build relationships and/or trust in the leader. While these clusters make sense, many of the characteristics have relevance to more than one cluster and could be placed there. Additionally, while these are about leaders of schools of character, they are actually generic leadership strengths.

First, each of the clusters will be discussed, along with the corresponding characteristics (see Table 10.1). Following each cluster, a list of questions is provided either for self- or other-study, to assess the level of each of the characteristics that you or someone else has. This is followed by suggestions on professional leadership development and how to use the checklist.

- *Inner strengths of the leader.* There are eight inner strengths that characterize great character education leaders. In a sense, these come closest to defining the character of the leader.

(1) Effective leaders have to ask themselves if there is a *noble purpose* behind their work. Are you *called* to do what you do? Does it serve the greater good? What *is* your noble purpose? Noble purpose is a purpose that seeks the good and looks beyond what is good for the self to good that serves others and the world in which we live. One principal wrote a short statement of his educational philosophy—including his noble purpose—and sent it to every applicant for a teaching position in his school.

(2) The second inner strength is *humility*. Humility does not mean self-deprecation. Rather it entails understanding one's own strengths along with one's weaknesses. It is about accurate self-assessment. It is also about decentering. There is a famous quote that is often inaccurately attributed to C.S. Lewis, but may actually be from Ken Blanchard: "*Humility is not thinking less of yourself, but thinking of yourself less.*" The reason that humility is important to leaders is that it allows one to serve, because it provides the perspective and foundation to put others first, certainly to put others above feeding one's own ego. I often tell educators that, by relying solely on ourselves for solutions and ideas, we are wasting the brains of those around us, including the children, even the little ones. I call this problem the "brain drain." The default option for many educational staff when a leader does not demonstrate humility is to just defer to the principal's judgment. This can be seductive to leaders and lead to increased authoritarianism. Another critical piece of humility is to recognize that we are all flawed and fallible. Robert George of Princeton University articulated this nicely when he said,

We must all recognize that we hold beliefs that are false. We just do not know which ones they are. [So] we should value truth over our own opinions; that is, we should *want* to discover which beliefs are wrong.

(3) The third inner strength is *benevolence*. I struggled with where to place benevolence. Megan Tschannen-Moran includes it as a trust-building characteristic, so it could easily go in the third cluster: Relationships and trustworthiness. I put it as an inner strength because the core of it is a caring attitude, or what Clifton Taulbert calls a *nurturing attitude* in *Eight Habits of the Heart*. It is a general feeling of care toward the well-being of others. A way of being in the world. To be an effective educational leader means to value and accept all others. Leaders need to care about kids . . . deeply. But they also need to care about teachers and support staff and parents. Education is a service profession. To

serve well one needs to care authentically about those being served. Scot Danforth, an expert in special education, used to teach a graduate class to special education teachers, where the only assignment was an action research project. Each teacher was instructed to identify the student they liked the least (which, in most cases, turns out to be pretty easy to do) and then try to like them more (not make the kids more likeable, not change the kids, but change the teacher's heart about the kid) and journal the journey. But caring is not enough, because one needs the capacity to understand and relate to others as well. As Tom Kolditz of the Doerr Center at Rice University has said, leaders "need to see the world through the eyes of the people they are leading."

(4) The fourth inner strength is *ethical*. People vary in the degree to which morality or ethics is central to them. This too is a factor in trustworthiness, so it could have been listed in the third cluster. Moral identity is the degree to which being a morally good person is central to your sense of self. Do you truly aspire to be a moral person? Do you think you are? What is your motivation for doing right? Sometimes we do what is right for extrinsic reasons such as material rewards or social acceptance, but I hope we do it for goodness' sake, that is, because we value morality. Leaders need to lead with their right. Another way to think of this is the moral compass.

(5) The fifth inner strength is *moral courage*. Ethical means school leaders need to be driven by a clear commitment to ethics and morality. But often there are obstacles to doing the right thing. Therefore, they also need the courage to do the right thing in the face of fear and threats and other obstacles.

(6) The sixth inner strength is *gratitude*. Gratitude is a sense of appreciation for what you have and what you have been given. It is the opposite of entitlement, a sense that you have a right to have whatever you have and have been given, which is coupled with a sense of resentment and a focus on what you do not have. A nice thing about gratitude is that it helps improve important parts of our lives—such as work performance and personal relationships—and can help us deal with serious life challenges, according to Bob Emmons, author of *Gratitude Works!*

(7) The seventh is *honesty*. Being a leader who speaks truth is foundational to so much of what a leader needs to accomplish in general and as a leader of a school of character.

(8) The eighth and final inner strength is *forgiveness*. To forgive is more about one's inner self than it is about the person being forgiven. It is the motivation and capacity to give up one's anger at a real or perceived wrong, to unburden oneself of those poisonous feelings. Many leaders have told us how hard—but critical—it is to forgive those who truly make it hard to fulfill your noble purpose, such as chronically complaining or uncooperative parents, frequent flyers, undermining nay-saying staff, and manipulative unjust bosses.

Reflection Questions for Leadership Inner Strengths

Noble Purpose

- Do you have a clear vision for the kind of school you want to shepherd?
- Is your vision explicitly grounded in clearly articulated values that you consider important?
- Is it focused on goodness, both at the individual level (moral character development of students, for example) and at the communal level (doing good in the world)?

- Do you articulate and share the vision?
- Are you open to feedback and improvement on your vision?

Humility

- Do you put the good of the school before yourself?
- Do you focus on others; i.e., do you listen to others, do you care about the well-being of others, etc.?
- Do you admit your mistakes or lack of knowledge, or are you defensive and try to cover up?
- Do you tell the truth even when it puts you in a bad light?
- Do you take responsibility for the consequences of your actions, policies, and decisions?
- Do you seek help when you need it?
- Do you recognize and rely on others for strengths that they have and that you do not?

Benevolence

- Do you invest resources (time, money, policy, structures) into taking care of all members of the school community?
- Are the feelings of others important to you?
- Do you authentically care about others? Even the challenging and less likeable others?
- Do you love kids? Even the "frequent flyers" who are often in trouble for misbehaviors?
- Do you recognize that all of us are imperfect?
- Can you avoid being judgmental of others who stumble? Do you see weakness in others as a failing?

Ethical

- Do you have a moral compass; is your life directed toward doing what is good and right?
- Is being good more important to you than winning?
- Do you follow the Golden Rule (or the Platinum Rule: Do unto others as they would want you to do unto them)?
- Do you consider the consequences of your actions and decisions on others, particularly on their welfare and rights?
- Do you intervene when you see a wrong being perpetrated?
- Can you resist peer pressure, tradition, authority, and/or popular opinion to do what is right?

Moral Courage

- When tough moral challenges are confronted, do you have the strength to take them on?
- Are you willing to suffer for what is right?
- Can you make the hard decisions, and own them and stick to them?
- Does your staff feel that they can trust you to do what is right, when it is hard to do so?
- Does your staff believe you will have their backs when they are right?

- Do you speak your mind, your truth, even if it is not popular?
- Are you willing to step out of your comfort zone, even put yourself at risk, to do what is right?

Gratitude

- Do you feel grateful for your life?
- Do you feel grateful for your job?
- Do you feel grateful for the people around you?
- Do you let people know you are grateful for them?
- Do you see the glass as half full and not half empty?
- Do you regularly send thank you notes to staff, students, parents, and others?
- Do you make a daily list of things for which you are grateful?
- Do you encourage others in the school to do likewise or even create structures and practices for them to reflect on and express their gratitude?

Honesty

- Do you value truth over harmony and popularity?
- Do you strive to tell what you believe to be true?
- Is it important to you when others do or do not tell the truth?

Forgiveness

- Do you recognize anger at others as an impediment to your well-being and your effectiveness?
- Do you work to unburden yourself of anger at others?
- Are you able to find constructive ways to move forward from injustices and unwarranted obstacles?
- Can you have healthy relationships with people who have wronged you?

- *Promoting the development of individuals and organizations.* There are four leadership strengths that support the focus on and promotion of the development of organizations and the individuals who populate them.

(1) The first is being *challenging*. Schools are progressive institutions. They are about learning and growing. Moving forward as a person. As Avis Glaze has said, educators "are in the people changing business." It is true both for children and

Table 10.1 Leadership Strengths

Inner Strengths	Promoting Development	Relational Trustworthiness
Noble Purpose	Challenging	Openness
Humility	Enriching	Authenticity
Benevolence	Foresight	Competence
Ethical	Stewardship	Inspirational
Moral Courage		Empowerment
Gratitude		Reliability
Honesty		
Forgiveness		

for adults. Julie Frugo's notion of the Professional Growth Leader is about a style of leadership that is devoted to creating an adult culture that promotes becoming one's best and most competent professional self. One critical way is to make the school productively challenging for all, including the adults. Being challenging is at the intersection of many of these strengths. Leaders who are also ethical and inspirational can more easily challenge others and push them harder. Hal Urban had a sign in his high school classroom that recommended "no parking in your comfort zone." Ron Berger often asks, "Is this your best work?" Leaders should have the same philosophy for their staff.

(2) The second growth-supportive characteristic is to be *enriching*. We all need new learning and, as we just saw, challenges in life to grow and flourish. It is the leader's role to model enrichment by providing new opportunities and roles and resources. There is a saying that "you need to feed the teachers so they don't eat the children." There is deep truth to feeding the minds and spirits of all stakeholders. Providing quality professional development is a key way to enrich and feed the staff.

(3) The third characteristic is *foresight*. K. Warner Schaie, many years ago, posited stages of adult intellectual development. He claimed that a hallmark of adult thinking was the capacity to think long term and to monitor progress over time. This applies not just to individuals but to organizational development too. This is particularly relevant to organizational leaders such as principals. We need leaders who have a long-term vision, for oneself, the individual members of the school community, and for the whole community. They also need to monitor progress of the development of the school along that long timeline. Market-driven societies, like the US, think in short-term impacts and indicators: What was the bottom line in the last quarter? Schools do not work that way. We often try to get kids to think about the consequences of their actions before they act. This is of the same ilk but much longer term and taking the perspective of an entire organization into account.

(4) The fourth growth-supportive characteristic is *stewardship*. There is a thought experiment called "the commons dilemma." A small group of people is told that they are residents in a hypothetical town and that their food is limited to the fish in the local pond. They are told that if they collectively take no more than 15 fish a day, the fish will continue to populate the pond, but if they collectively take more than 15, then the population of fish will decline until there is no more food for their children and grandchildren, etc. Then each person privately "fishes"; that is, each individual indicates how many fish he or she will take the first day. And the next. And the next. In very few cycles, most groups exhaust all the fish and wipe out the entire town, if not for their generation, then for the next. This is the opposite of stewardship and clearly relates to many environmental challenges we are all facing. Unless you are opening a new school or closing a school, you are but part of a chain of people who have led or will lead the school. Each school leader is being given the great responsibility of all the people in the school, especially the children, and the school itself, now and into the future. Tom Kolditz has said that, "the focus in training leaders is not the impact on the leaders, but the impact on the people she or he leads, now or later." You should recognize the role of foresight, empowerment, and servant leadership in stewardship. Your stewardship for that which is put in your trust should be salient, motivating, and deeply felt. It is a profound and sacred trust, a great responsibility. We all stand on the shoulders of the giants who came before us, which is why we can see further than they did. We all create ripples in the pond of life. We need leaders who understand that and take that responsibility very seriously.

Reflection Questions on How Leaders Strive to Develop Individuals and Organizations

Challenging

- Do you present questions and experiences for others that will challenge them and help them grow?
- Do you see the possibilities in others and act to make them more likely?
- Do you create an environment where people will have to take on new tasks and roles? Do you scaffold such experiences and situations?
- Do you model and support experiential pedagogies for students? Do you do the same for staff?
- Are you okay with failure, and have you created a safe culture where staff and students are not afraid to fail?
- Do you encourage and support staff in earning degrees and certificates and taking on new and challenging roles?

Enriching

- Do you prioritize innovation, especially toward enriching the learning and developmental contexts in the school?
- Do you focus on the professional growth of your staff?
- Do you lead book studies and other study groups with staff?
- Do you seek newer and better methods and structures?
- Do you lead in ways that will contribute to the flourishing of others and the world in which we live?
- Do you strategically bring to the school new ideas that will enrich the culture, methods, and outcomes of the school?

Foresight

- Do you care deeply about the future, beyond yourself?
- Are you passionate about, do you advocate for, and do you act to support broad issues such as peace, environmental health, the moral messages we send to children, etc.?
- Do you think and plan about how you will fulfill your responsibility for the long-term flourishing of the school (even after you have left the school)?
- Do you embrace "*Tikkun Olam*" (to heal the world) by devoting yourself to the long-term improvement of that which you have been given responsibility?
- Do you have a sustainability plan for the school?
- Do you look for future leaders among your staff?

Stewardship

- Do you have a strategic plan?
- Is it long-term?
- Do you regularly/periodically monitor progress?
- Do you feel responsible for the long-term well-being of the school?
- Do you have a clear sense of the steps along the journey for your strategic goals?

- *Relational/Trustworthy*. The third cluster of leadership characteristics entails six strengths that support relationship building and a sense of the leader's trustworthiness. As we shall see in the next section of the book, Relationships, the R in PRIMED, are critical to effective schools and character education. And we shall also see that collegial trust enhances school climate, academic achievement, and character development. Of particular importance is the staff's sense of the school leader's trustworthiness.

(1) The first relational/trustworthiness strength is *openness*. Some people are very transparent; they wear their feelings on their sleeves. They have little hesitancy to allow others to know them. We all know people who are "open books" and others who are closed off from us. Good leaders need to be comfortable with themselves, willing to be vulnerable, and willing to authentically share themselves with those they lead and other school stakeholders. Of course this needs to be a measured judgment, because the principal sets the emotional tone for the school, and there may be times where a more moderated demeanor will serve the greater good.

(2) The second relational/trustworthiness strength is *authenticity*. Parker Palmer, in *The Courage to Teach*, focuses on the necessity to be true to oneself. He claims you cannot be an excellent educator if you do not know yourself—an ancient Confucian virtue—and then teach from your authentic self. Socrates taught that self-knowledge is the beginning of wisdom. A leader needs to lead from her authentic self. It is critical to dig deep into who one truly is, why you chose to lead, and how you can best serve those you lead. Authenticity can also be understood as a form of integrity, something many of you may have as a school core value or virtue. Stephen Carter, in his book *Integrity*, identifies its three elements: (a) Figuring out what is right and wrong; (b) doing what you then know is right (even if there is a cost to doing so); (c) openly admitting that you are acting to do what you know is right. Another window into understanding integrity is that it comes from the Latin root for the word integer. Its roots are in the concept of oneness, singularity, unity. It refers to a unity of your values, words, and deeds. Integrity essentially is what Tom Lickona often suggests: Practice what you preach, but do not forget to preach what you practice. Trust is critical to effective leadership. People cannot trust you if you are not authentic and do not demonstrate integrity. Robert George cautions that integrity is sadly rare, but that we should both "embrace the inevitable fallibility of all, especially ourselves" and "recognize the rare instances of integrity in others, especially when we disagree with them." In essence, he is wedding humility and authenticity.

(3) The third element of this cluster is *Competence*. Staff trust the leader to the degree that they perceive the leader as competent at her job and generally as an educator. While this can apply to all the tasks and competencies of a school leader, for our purposes it has largely to do with core character education leadership tasks, such as managing the adult culture, guiding and modeling a developmental behavior management philosophy and system, and providing professional guidance on relevant professional development.

(4) The fourth element is *inspirational*. I have known many low key and soft-spoken principals who were excellent as school leaders, particularly leaders of schools of character. Being inspirational is about what others do because of you, not what you do. Do others follow, emulate, and admire you? To be an effective leader, others have to follow you. It is helpful to differentiate a charismatic leader

from an inspirational leader. The former is always liked and may be respected; the latter is always respected and may be liked.

(5) The fifth relational/trustworthiness characteristic is *Empowerment*. Excellent, caring educators can also be, in effect, dictators. They may be benevolent dictators but dictators nonetheless. It is the rarer case that an educator intuitively shares power and control in any meaningful or significant way. Since Empowerment is the E in PRIMED and will be discussed in depth later, we will say no more about it here, other than that empowering others is a form of respect for them and helps builds relationships.

(6) The last of the six relational/trustworthiness characteristics is *Reliability*. A central element in trusting someone is knowing you can depend on him or her. Part of that is being transparent (open, authentic), but another piece is predictability. Is the leader likely to do what they say they will and what you expect they will? Can you count on it?

Reflection Questions on How Leaders Build Relationships and Trust

Openness

- Do you welcome input?
- Do you solicit input?
- Do you reflect on and seriously consider input when you receive it? Are you willing to change?
- Do you value innovation, new ideas, and creativity?
- Are you flexible (not rigid)?
- Do you seek opinions that are different from your own?

Authenticity

- Do you practice what you preach?
- Are you the same person regardless of whom you are with?
- Do people feel they can trust you?
- Do you consistently live by your principles?
- Are you reflective (not impulsive)?
- Do you know yourself well; are you introspective?
- Do people have a clear sense of who you are, what you value, and why you do what you do?
- Do you intentionally let others know your motives and deeds?

Competence

- Are you good at understanding others?
- Are you effective at building, maintaining and restoring healthy relationships with others?
- Do you know how to and do you model effective ways to work with others to improve their behaviors?
- Do you model personal/professional growth, and are you able to motivate others to develop and grow?
- Do others see you as a competent leader?

Inspirational

- Do others want to follow you?
- Do you motivate others to join your noble purpose?
- Do others look up to you and emulate you?
- Can you change others' behavior simply by being or doing what you want them to be or do?
- Do you bring out the best in others?

Empowerment

- Do you share power with others?
- Do you encourage teachers to share power with students and to create classrooms that are more democratic?
- Do you authentically delegate authority to others?
- Do you listen?
- Do you have a collaborative leadership style?
- Are you willing to "lose" debates and disagreements?

Reliability

- Do you try to keep promises and meet deadlines?
- Do people feel they can count on you to deliver what is promised or expected?
- Are you seen as predictable and consistent?

● ● ● ● ●

Professional Development for School Leaders in Character Education

For more than two decades, I have been providing deep and sustained professional development to school leaders, mainly in the St. Louis region. Most of this work is through our Leadership Academy in Character Education or LACE (https://characterandcitizenship.org/programs/leadership-academy). Every year, since 1998, we accept a cohort (or two) of approximately 30–35 school leaders into LACE. Then we provide them with a yearlong series of professional growth experiences. Most of LACE is built on two such elements. First, most of the monthly full-day meetings are workshops by some of the leading thinkers in character education, most of whom you will hear about at various points in this book. They include Tom Lickona, Hal Urban, Clifton Taulbert, Avis Glaze, Ron Berger, and Phil Vincent, among others. The second key element is the curriculum. Each LACE participant is required to assemble (or redesign) a site-based character education team, and each month they are assigned a reflection assignment to be done as a team. In this way, we are introducing collaborative leadership to our approach. The assignments vary widely and include subjects such as increasing stakeholder buy-in, an assessment plan, a variation on a SWOT (strengths, weaknesses, opportunities, threats) analysis, and an analysis of key elements in character education in their school. Most importantly, they submit this in writing and receive individual constructive/critical feedback from one of the LACE directors, which they take back to their team, consider, and integrate into the written document. Additional LACE elements are site visits to exemplary schools, a starter library of key books, and monthly "morning meetings" for sharing. Approximately 30 such cohorts have experienced LACE in St. Louis to this point, and five more have done so in other locations (Kansas City, Milwaukee).

LACE has also generated other opportunities for leader professional development. The HTC Education Foundation in Taiwan has funded a video-based blended learning version of LACE, which they are now translating into Chinese but which can be used in other places and other ways either in the existing English form or by translation (we are about to translate and use it in Spanish, through a grant from the Templeton World Charity Foundation). There are nine full day workshops in this format, including videos of the LACE presenters, facilitator's guide, group activities, and the LACE curriculum. We now also have funding from the John Templeton Foundation to integrate the work of Dr. Melinda Bier (described earlier) in servant leadership into LACE and to create freestanding professional development modules about servant leadership as well. The Kern Family Foundation has funded us to create a post-LACE mentoring element in which LACE graduates will receive approximately one to two years of on-site mentoring by current or former principals who themselves have been recognized for excellence in leading schools of character.

At the suggestion of LACE graduates, we created the weeklong PRIMED Institute in Character Education (PICE; https://characterandcitizenship.org/programs/summer-institute). which we have offered for a decade and a half in St. Louis and, again with the support of the HTC Educational Foundation, for nearly a decade in Taiwan. The Templeton World Charity Foundation has funded CoSchool in Colombia to establish a PICE in Bogotá in 2019 and 2020 and will also fund one in Jalisco Mexico by Panamerican University in 2021. PICE has three main goals: (1) one-week immersion in character education; (2) team building; (3) character education strategic planning.

While we do not have data on the impact of LACE in the St. Louis region, we can extrapolate from some other data. We do not know the exact number of schools in the St. Louis region, but there are slightly over 2,000 schools in the state of Missouri. This accounts for approximately 2% of all the schools in the US (almost 100,000). The St. Louis region therefore accounts for less than 2% of all US schools. Yet St. Louis accounts for nearly one out of every four National Schools of Character, and schools led by a head principal who has graduated from LACE account for almost one in five of all NSOCs in the entire country. Supporting the deep professional development of school leaders and centering it on character education makes a profound difference in the quality of the schools. Soon, thanks to the John Templeton Foundation, we will have empirical evidence on the impact of our LACE plus servant leadership model we call CEEL. It is also worth repeating that deep evidence-based character education also enhances academic achievement. It is a win-win-win.

● ● ● ● ●

Tips on Using the Questions for Each Leadership Characteristic

There are questions at the end of each of the leadership clusters that you could use in various ways:

- Simply answer them for yourself, as a self-reflection activity
- Rate yourself on each question from 1 to 5:
    1—Never or almost never.
    2—Sometimes but not often.

3—Periodically, sometimes.
4—Frequently.
5—Always or almost always.

- Use them to rate another person, either by simply answering them or by using the rating scale.
- Have a group of people (the school staff, for example) engage in a self-rating, and then perhaps discuss as a group the insights people gleaned from doing this.
- Ask your staff to rate you using the rating scale, and then compile the results. If you are very brave (remember, courage is one of our leadership virtues), present the summed results to the staff and discuss them together.
- Do a 360-degree procedure where you rate yourself, your supervisor rates you, and those you supervise rate you. Then compare the results, and ideally discuss them with others.
- Use the results of any of these procedures to identify strengths and areas for growth. Then create a strategic plan for personal improvement based on the results. What specific characteristics do you want to work on? Create SMART goals (specific, measurable, achievable, relevant, and timely). You can find many SMART goal worksheet templates on the web. Consider having an "accountability buddy" to check in periodically to help monitor your progress and keep you on track.

Resources for Prioritization

Books

Bryk, A., & Schneider, B. (2002). *Trust in Schools: A Core Resource for Improvement*. New York: Russell Sage Foundation.

Damon, W. (2009). *The Path to Purpose: How Young People Find Their Calling in Life*. New York: Free Press.

Emmons, Robert (2013). *Gratitude Works! A 21-Day Program for Creating Emotional Prosperity*. San Francisco: Jossey-Bass.

Enright, Robert (2015). *8 Keys to Forgiveness*. New York: W.W. Norton.

Malin, Heather (2018). *Teaching for Purpose: Preparing Students for Lives of Meaning*. Cambridge, MA: Harvard Education Press.

Responsive Classroom (2015). *The First Six Weeks of school* (2nd Edition). Turner Falls, MA: Center for Responsive Schools.

Tschannen-Moran, Megan (2014). *Trust Matters: Leadership for Successful Schools* (2nd Edition). New York: Wiley.

Urban, Hal (2008). *Lessons from the Classroom: 20 Things Good Teachers Do*. Redwood City, CA: Great Lessons Press.

Websites

www.characterlab.org
www.evworthington-forgiveness.com/
www.greatergood.com
https://internationalforgiveness.com/

PRIMED Action Planning Worksheet:

Prioritization Strategies

Prioritization: Ensuring that character education as a strategy and character development as an outcome is an authentic (explicit, supported) priority for the school/district.

Evidence-based implementation strategies:

Rhetoric: Core values/Shared goals/Common language

Resources: Leadership allocation of resources to character education

Intentionally creating a learning community

Investing in professional development for character education

Climate: Safe environment

Assess school culture/climate

Trust in teachers

School-wide character education culture/focus

Caring classroom/school climate

Structures: Comprehensive approach to character education

School displays/awards

Clear rules

Assessment and feedback for character/SEL

Inter-school collaboration

Leadership: Principal competently leads the initiative

STEP ONE:

Please identify at least two prioritization strategies that are already in place in your school/district. You may use the previous categories or anything else you do that you think increases the centrality of character education for your school's purpose and functioning.

1.

2.

3.

4.

STEP TWO:

Please identify at least two more things you can do that would increase the prioritization of character education and character development in your school/district. Again, you can choose from the previous list or list anything else you think would be good to implement for the purpose of increased emphasis and support of character education.

1.

2.

3.

4.

Part III

PRIMED Principle 2: Relationships

11

•••••

Why Relationships?

Relationships are the foundational and critical building blocks of effective schools, character education, and character development. They comprise one of the three fundamental human needs according to Self-determination Theory, which informs many excellent character education initiatives. That is why they define the second Design Principle of PRIMED after the meta-principle of Prioritization. Relationships need to be an authentic priority for character education to be successful, indeed for schools to be successful overall.

In this chapter we explore why relationship building needs to be a priority and then, in the next chapter, the specific evidence-based practices for fostering the development of healthy relationships among stakeholders *within* the school. In the third chapter in this section, we will examine relationships with those stakeholders *outside* the school.

Long ago, based on decades of work with educators, I concluded that almost all educators come to education with golden hearts ... for children. They truly want what is best for students, and they authentically want to help shepherd their journeys toward learning and flourishing. They choose the profession in order to serve the best developmental and academic interests of children, and that includes having healthy relationships with them and nurturing healthy relationships between children.

Unfortunately, with the best intentions they sometimes implement strategies that are ineffective or even counterproductive. And they assume their golden hearts are sufficient for healthy relationships to develop. They are essentially right; if you authentically care about children, then those relationships will indeed develop ... except for those children who need additional healthy relationships the most and may in fact resist such relationships as Marilyn Watson points out so well in *Learning to Trust*. And this is also true of (1) adults in the school, (2) children with emotional challenges or who are merely shy ... or different, (3) children with low self-esteem, (4) children of trauma, (5) children with unhealthy attachment histories, (6) newcomers to the school, (7) and those in the school who most frequently are marginalized, such as the "non-professional" staff (cooks, secretaries, custodians, etc.). One cannot truly be a community if only some members of the community are included or respected. The real trick here is for relationship building to be comprehensive and inclusive. It must include all in the school and ideally stakeholders outside the school as well, especially those for whom such relationships are less likely and more needed. And to do so, *relationship building (for all) needs to be an authentic, intentional, and strategic focus of the school*. It needs to be a priority, which is why Prioritization is the first element of PRIMED.

One aphorism for educators that we introduced earlier is very relevant here: "Kids don't care how much you know until they know how much you care." How often have we heard our own kids tell us, "I *love* algebra/literature/European History (etc.)" when they have historically hated that subject? Why? They *love* the teacher they now have for that subject. Relationships are the molecules from which we build both great schools and good character. Therefore, we have to nurture those relationships strategically and intentionally. We cannot simply assume they will happen.

Let us start this exploration on the other end of the lifespan. There is a lot of research on the correlates of having a successful and fulfilling late adulthood. It includes some obvious things like not smoking, keeping your weight in a healthy range, not abusing alcohol, and exercising regularly. But the list includes some things you may not have thought of, such as continually learning new things. Another is to have a companion in late adulthood. Many people in late adulthood have suffered significant social loss, including widowhood. Their set of close relationships, particularly peer relationships, is likely to be greatly diminished if not erased completely. It is impossible to make new "old friends"; that is, friends with whom you have a substantial history. Now such a companion does not have to be a marital partner or even an intimate partner of any sort. It can simply be a good friend or even a roommate. The point is to have someone on whom you can rely and whom you can trust (trust will be a repeated theme in this book) and with whom you can share the rhythms, challenges, and activities of life. Social isolation is a threat to well-being.

Marilyn Watson does a great job of applying attachment theory to education, and we will explore that more in the sections on Intrinsic Motivation and on Developmental Pedagogy. Essentially, attachment theory says that, for many species including humans, infant bonding to a caretaker (or caretakers) is an evolutionary mechanism necessary for healthy development. In humans, this kicks into high gear about midway through the first year of life and stays paramount through the first few years of life. However, it remains part of who we are and continues to develop throughout our lives. In fact, Erik Erikson talks about our relationships with our parents as important in our own late lives, even after our parents have long since passed on. They live on in our hearts and minds, and our relationship with them continues to influence who we are and how we live.

Here is how attachment works its magic. If we have consistent, responsive, and nurturing interactions with a primary caretaker (or more than one), usually but not necessarily one's biological parent, then we develop a basic framework that the world is safe and predictable and nurturing, which we generalize not only to all people but also to animals and even inanimate objects. We experience the world around us through a lens of trust and optimism. However, if our early relational experiences are chaotic and unpredictable, neglectful of our needs and distress signals, harsh and hurtful, or in other ways inappropriate, then we develop a general sense of the world as threatening— and people, animals, and things as something to avoid and fear. We then experience the world around us through a lens of mistrust and pessimism. No less than our entire personalities and ways of engaging the world for the rest of our lives are at stake here. This is a big deal. Relationships are critical to well-being on both the front end and back end of life, and their ripples hit almost all aspects of our lives.

Another interesting insight into relationships is what forms them. A wonderful model of marital relationships describes the decision to marry (or form any committed relationship) as often based on passing a series of relational filters. First is proximity, so that you have to have contact to start the relationship, which is now far easier with web networking. Other filters are attraction, enjoying each other's company, having compatible beliefs and values, etc. I often teach educators that the two ingredients in forming relationships in school are learning about each other and having positive experiences with each other, even laughing together. These are clearly things teachers can try to make happen. We will explore how to do so in the next chapter.

Some of the bases for building healthy relationships are listed here. Each of these can be the rationale and blueprint for designing experiences in the classroom and/or school that increase the likelihood of healthy relationships forming.

- *Listening to each other*: As we shall see in the Empowerment section—and as Self-determination Theory teaches us—everyone has a fundamental need for their voice to matter and to be authentically heard by others.
- *Learning about each other*: Knowledge of the other is foundational, so sharing, inquiring, and disclosing are important.
- *Having fun experiences together*: We come to like and accept people more if we have had fun together and laughed together.
- *Working together* (ideally on something meaningful): Having been jointly productive is another basis for forming a relationship.

An important addendum to relationships is collaboration. In the next two chapters, we will explore both relationships with others in general—and true collaboration with them as well. To authentically and effectively collaborate, we should:

- *Communicate effectively*: Collaboration requires accurate understanding of the other's knowledge, skills, motives, strategies, and values.
- *Serve the other*: Collaboration is optimized when the collaborators are functioning optimally; one way to ensure that is to serve one's fellow collaborators in ways that support their optimal functioning.
- *Empower the other*: Wasting a fellow collaborator's talents by hand-cuffing them in some way undermines optimal collaboration, so empowering them to do what they can do to contribute to the collaboration (and respecting their potential and capacity) is foundational to collaboration.
- *Work as equals*: Optimally collaboration is egalitarian, a true balanced partnership.

Relationships are critical to our well-being. And our well-being is critical to our success in life, including in school. And they are formative of who we become. They shape us and leave an indelible mark on us. The word character after all comes from the Greek work referring to the unique mark on something, as the mark on a coin. As we have already noted, Self-determination Theory highlights "belonging" or connectedness as one of their three fundamental human needs or motives. Relationships therefore fulfill a fundamental human need.

We have just explored some disparate snapshots of the centrality of relationships to human flourishing. Now we will turn to what this looks like in schools, relying heavily, as we will do throughout this book, on what research tells us works well in schools to build character in students.

12

●●●●●

Relationships in School

When we think about nurturing relationships in education, we need to think broadly. We certainly want to focus on relationships students have, either with each other or with their teachers. That is the low-hanging fruit, the obvious stuff, albeit critical to school health, effectiveness, and character development. But we also have to think more broadly, which includes thinking beyond the physical boundaries of the school and to a broader set of school stakeholder categories. Hence, we will also look at relationships among the teaching staff, between administrators and teachers, with support staff, and even with connected community members, of course including parents and other caretakers. Many students are not raised by parents, certainly not always biological parents. For the sake of simplicity in writing, however, when we talk about children's parents we mean to include biological, adoptive, and stepparents, as well other legal guardians and surrogate parents. In this and the next chapter, we will offer specific examples of such relationship-building strategies. In this chapter, we will focus on relationships within the school and in the next chapter on relationships with stakeholders external to the school.

●●●●●

Teacher-to-Student Relationships

As Eric Schaps, founding Executive Director of the Developmental Studies Center (now the Center for the Collaborative Classroom) in California has reminded us, students do not come to school worrying about the curriculum ("I wonder what new vocabulary words we will learn this year?"). Rather, they come to school worrying about how they will get along with others ("I hope people are nice to me"), and this includes the new teachers they get each year. It is important to note that the US tends to operate a bit differently than most other countries in this regard. US schools tend to reassign teachers and students each year, so students start each year with a lot of social uncertainty.

Remember the aphorism, "Kids don't care how much you know until they know how much you care"? Well an addendum to that is that you are not likely to fool them into believing you care about them if you really do not. It is a human survival strategy; people need to be able to discern sincere from insincere concern. They need to know who they can and cannot rely upon, to trust, to have their backs. We all do. When my son was entering his second year of schooling, Lake Bluff Elementary in Shorewood WI (later recognized as a National School of Character) had two years of half-day kindergarten, K4 and K5. He had lucked out in K4, getting a master teacher who had been delaying retirement until her granddaughter could be in her class. We were lucky that her granddaughter entered school the same year Danny did, and they were both assigned to the same class. It was readily apparent why she was deemed a master teacher and was so highly lauded. She was truly amazing. And it was a great year for him, for us, and for all his classmates.

The next year he was assigned one of the two K5 teachers. Other parents warned us that we would not like his teacher. They said she was a "cold fish." Not warm, effervescent, and loving like his K4 teacher. As parents going through this for the first time, we became nervous, wary, and worried about our poor darling boy suffering a year with a heartless cold fish of a teacher. At first, this older, very reserved and controlled teacher made me think of the stereotype of the austere and strict frontier "school marm." Our concerns deepened and we considered asking the principal, Kirk Juffer (a truly superb school leader, who over his long tenure in the school built a brilliant and successful school focusing on student development) to switch Danny to the other K5 teacher. We did not want to be helicopter parents, however and delayed intervening. Actually, his teacher turned out to be a great teacher. She was excellent pedagogically and at classroom management. More importantly, she loved the kids, in her own quiet, undemonstrative, but dependable way. And the kids knew it, and they flourished. She just happened to be awkward with parents (perhaps all adults), but that was irrelevant to the experience of her students. Relationships and love: The kids need them and they will know if they are real, regardless of whether the teacher wears it on her sleeve or does it subtly and in ways that may be less obvious. Kids' "care radar" will detect authentic love and concern, or the lack of it.

When my son was in high school, I was asked to serve on a district-wide strategic planning committee focusing on character education. On the committee were school staff, parents, and a few high school students. At one meeting, a parent asked the students, "If you had a serious problem at school, is there someone you could go to for help?" One girl started to answer and suddenly seemed to have an epiphany, stopped in mid reply, and, looking very confused and surprised, she asked the querying parent, in an astonished and cynical tone, "You mean an adult?!" It was clear that she had not even considered adults when she first began to answer. Apparently, it was too far-fetched to her to even imagine that you could trust the adults in the school with a personal problem. I took that as a powerful condemnation of the state of teacher–student relationships in her school, which in fact was a good school with high academic achievement but was missing the mark on fostering the flourishing of human goodness. I firmly believe that if the two boys who did the shootings at Columbine High School in the late 1990s had each had a healthy relationship with an adult in the school, it is likely that no one would have died that day. In fact, Katherine Newman, in her book *Rampage*, identifies five characteristics of students who engage in school shootings. Two of them are: (1) marginalized by peers and (2) very rigid parameters for being accepted by peers. It should be obvious how relationships and school climate can ameliorate both of these. And remember, the goal of the two student shooters at Columbine was not to kill just a few people; they had attempted to bring enough explosives to the school to kill everyone in the building. Relationships save lives. I have seen it repeatedly.

As I have said, relationship-building needs to be intentional and strategic. Opportunities need to be built into the schedule and structure of the day/week/semester/year. Educators need to be intentional and proactive about fostering relationships. This is just as true of teacher-to-student relationships as it is regarding student-to-student relationships.

We have seen that one key element of relationships is knowledge of each other. Many school staff, especially elementary schools, either mandate or simply suggest teachers contact students before the school year starts. Some even do home visits to get to know the students and their families, to build relationships with them, and to learn a bit more about the context from which each kid comes to school every day.

Others create surveys on their students and gather important information, either from their parents or, when the kids are old enough, from the kids themselves. Hal Urban used a detailed survey he gave to all his high school students, which he often used to start conversations, to find shared interests, or in other ways to support the building or enhancing of relationships with them. Remember, relationships come from learning about each other plus having positive experiences with each other. This certainly comes from the "learning about" side, but it can be done in fun and interesting ways. We will see more examples of this when we discuss student–student relationships, ways that can apply to teacher–student relationships as well.

This notion of getting to know kids right off the bat relies on my belief that *beginnings are sacred*. First impressions are a good example of that. Many future and new teachers are told cynically, "don't smile until Christmas" (which comes about half way through the school year in the US). That is simply horrible advice. The idea, I think, is to set the classroom discipline bar very high so you can ease off a bit as the year goes on. But it ignores the fact that students will not perform optimally, either academically or behaviorally, if they do not feel loved and respected, if they do not experience their need for "belongingness," one of the three pillars of Self-determination Theory, being met.

The exact opposite of putting on a cold, uncaring demeanor is letting them know you care right away and starting on that critical relationship immediately. Clifton Taulbert tells the story of his first day of school, in a segregated school in the rural cotton-farming Mississippi Delta. He was petrified and did not want to go. His teacher took his hand at the door and said, "Come on in, little professor." He found her to be loving and caring, and he quickly got over his fears and loved school, ultimately graduating as the valedictorian of his high school class. How might this have gone if this great teacher heeded the advice not to smile before Christmas?

Learning about another is not a one-way street. Students want to know about the adults in their lives, especially their teachers. In *Educating for Character*, Tom Lickona reports on a brilliant strategy designed by Kim McConnell at Walt Disney Elementary School in San Ramon, California. Rather than doing what most teachers do at the beginning of the year, in other words preparing and delivering an autobiographical presentation of some sort to the students, this innovative teacher started the year by inviting the students to interview her about anything they wanted to know. Furthermore, she asked them to take notes on every question she was asked and every answer she gave. Then they were assigned to go home and write her biography. And it was collected for academic credit . . . but only if it had been read to an adult in the student's family.

There are so many best practices of character education (and many academic ones as well) in this simple lesson that it is hard to list them all. Primarily, the focus is on students getting to know their teacher. Then there are plenty of academic goals being met as well; learning about biography, listening, formulating questions, public speaking, note-taking, vocabulary, spelling, etc. Most important for character education however is that this teacher flipped the power structure in the classroom to empower (the E in PRIMED) the students to be in charge of her and the lesson. They decided what to learn about her. Then, again brilliantly, she threw in parental involvement, building a relationship between the teacher and the parent. Parents learned right away that they were expected to be part of what students learned in school. And they got to learn a bit about their child's new teacher right away, one of our foundations of relationship building. Simply brilliant.

Many schools start the day with teachers greeting students. They are stationed in the hallways and high-five and engage the students as they work their way through this gantlet of love on the way to their classrooms. At An Achievable Dream Academy in Newport News, Virginia, not only are the teachers there, but a bus load of military personnel from a local US Army base also come every morning to help greet the kids. These kids, predominantly under-resourced (and many at-risk) kids, are greeted enthusiastically by multiple adults before they arrive at their classrooms. The Army personnel could be heard not only greeting the students, but also greeting them by name, frequently asking personal questions or making personalized comments. "Nice new hair cut! Looks good on you, Maria." "How's the puppy, Leon? Keeping you guys up at night?" Etc.

A practice that seems to be growing in popularity is teachers greeting kids at the classroom door. Hal Urban began doing that over 50 years ago with his high school students and found it to be the single easiest and most powerful innovation among all his creative and brilliant initiatives in the classroom. He began with handshakes but then realized high school students do not typically shake hands when greeting each other, so he expanded to whatever the individual student preferred (another form of Empowerment), such as high fives, hugs, and "secret" handshakes. Many elementary school teachers use some variations of the "3 Hs": Handshake, hug or high-five. For the little ones, some teachers sit on a chair at the door to be on eye level with the students. One teacher at An Achievable Dream Academy said that she looks in the kids' eyes and can quickly see if something might be awry as they arrive and can then have a side discussion with them to salvage what might otherwise turn into a disrupted, disruptive, and unproductive day. The title of my last book, *You Can't Teach Through a Rat*, comes from the idea that kids come with stuff on their minds and you will not be able to reach or teach them that day if you do not deal with it. Another variation on individual greetings is to do this as a departure mechanism at dismissal time.

Creating the time to spend time with each student individually is another way to invest in teacher–student relationships. Of course, this has to be for all students, both so it is not seen as favoritism and so that those who are least likely to develop healthy relationships get the opportunity. I was doing a workshop at Azusa Pacific University many years ago. After my talk, a man approached me. He said he taught ten-year-olds and wanted my advice about one of his students. She was largely inert, not talking in class, not doing her work, etc. He claimed he had tried everything to reach her. I love hearing "I've tried *everything*" because no one has and it is a great opportunity to identify a strategy that one has not yet tried. He told me she came from a dysfunctional family. As I began to ask a few more questions so I could reply more responsibly, he pulled a small piece of paper from his pocket. It was a note she had written to him. It was a beautifully, lovingly, intricately, and meticulously drawn heart with the message, "To Mr. Smith, my best friend." I was stunned. First, I was stunned that he actually felt he had not reached her, and second I was stunned because on some level he understood the importance of that note, enough at least to carry it around with him and show it to me. Clearly, he cared deeply about this little girl and wanted to improve his relationship with her. And clearly, she felt the same way about him. Therefore, I said, "What do you mean you haven't reached her? She not only has indicated that you have reached her, but she has told you how she wants to interact with you!" When he did not seem to get it, I said, "She wants to write. She wrote to you, now write back to her."

A different teacher in a Chicago high school for underserved and under-resourced high school boys, who were struggling to make it in school, once told me that he tells all his students, most of whom are reading and writing well below grade level expectations, that if they write to him he will write back. He found that many of his students were hesitant to open up about their struggles face to face but would open up in writing. In many ways, this parallels the story of Erin Gruell and *Freedom Writers*. This was well before the current status of the internet and social media, so this writing was on paper. Moreover, this Chicago teacher always answered every student. He reported that many more than he expected eagerly took him up on this offer and continued to communicate in writing. How much easier would it be today to do this electronically?

Finding common interests is another great way to build relationships. One school in Florida made the final hour of each day essentially an activity club, mostly around physical exercise. Teachers were required to propose a club around an activity or interest of their own and every student was able to join whichever club/activity interested them the most. Other schools broaden this to any activity (hobbies, etc.). Some schools do this as after-school activities. Others let students propose and, in many cases, teach the clubs, resulting in the teacher and student swapping roles. This does not need to be limited to certified (licensed) teachers. All school staff can either share their passions or learn from others. This can also have an informal structure. Hal Urban for instance would eat lunch in his classroom every day and let students know they were welcome to join him if they wanted. Other teachers join students in the student cafeteria for informal lunchtime conversations.

Some teachers go beyond the school day and physical environment to connect with students. I already mentioned the possibility of home visits at the beginning of the school year. Others do this to help students who are struggling. At Ridgewood Middle School in Arnold Missouri (a NSOC), then Principal and Assistant Principal, Tim Crutchley and Kristen Pelster, respectively, would go to truant students' homes and get them up and to school. Often parents would say they were unable to get their pre- and early teens to comply or to simply wake up or get out of bed in the morning, and they relished the authority and help of the school leaders. They were frequently deeply grateful for the help. Of course, this needs to be done in a safe and respectful way. For example, neither Pelster nor Crutchley ever did this alone; there were always two adults from the school on such "visits." This and other strategies were based on their philosophy that students could not succeed if they were not at school and did not do their work. Simple and smart.

This example stretches the boundaries of the teacher–student relationships, as it is about school leaders and not teachers. That, of course, is another critical relationship— but one we will not spend much time on as it is so similar to teacher–student relationships. However, it is important to mention at least a few examples. Franklin McCallie, a legendary former principal of Kirkwood High School in St. Louis, would photograph each student and study their pictures and names so he could address them all by name. Mike Hylen, former Principal of Francis Howell Union High School, a suburban alternative high school for students who were struggling in their traditional schools, stood in the doorway every day at dismissal and high-fived each of his approximately 100 students as they left at the end of the day. It was not uncommon for his students to stick their heads inside the door to the office and ask "Is Hylen in?" When the secretary said yes and asked if they needed to talk to him, they typically answered "no" and left. They apparently just felt better simply knowing that he was there. Other principals have small rotating "advisory committees" with whom they meet and sometimes have a special lunch to get their perspectives on—and advice for—the school . . . but mostly to build relationships.

One middle school in Minnesota, part of the Search Institute's 40 Developmental Assets model, had teachers identify every student with whom they had more than a "this student is in my class" relationship. Then they looked at all students in the school and identified those who had no such relationship with even a single teacher (no teacher had listed them). Then, assuming that these students were likely to be struggling at-risk students, they asked teachers to volunteer to form a relationship with one of those students who currently had no meaningful relationship with at least one teacher. They started making casual contact—noting a new haircut and so on— and slowly built deeper relationships, strategically and intentionally. At Karen Smith's school (Mark Twain Elementary, in St. Louis), their mascot was the Navigator (in honor of Mark Twain), and they had a structure called Navigator Pals. Any student who a staff member felt could benefit from an additional nurturing relationship with an adult was assigned to an adult in the school. All adults were included: The principal, the secretary, the teachers, the cook, etc. If a student was having a difficult time in class, the teacher did not have to resort to restricting, chastising, or punishing. She simply could say, "Would you like to go spend time with (the student's Navigator Pal)?" and then sent her to make a short visit, where she would be loved and heard by someone with whom she had a special relationship. Typically, five minutes later she was back in her classroom doing just fine.

These are but some ways of building relationships between students and school staff. Additional ones are limited only by your imagination and creativity. Students are thirsting for such relationships, so forming them is typically easy. The main point is to do it strategically and intentionally—often through formal school structures and schedules—and to be authentic and sustained. Moreover to include *all* students.

● ● ● ● ●

Student-to-Student Relationships

As noted earlier, kids need friends and especially at least one authentic, prosocial, healthy peer relationship, particularly as they move through middle childhood and onward. Despite the fact that many elementary school teachers address their students as "friends," in fact not all fellow students are likely to be one's friends. Regardless, relationships with *all* fellow students need to at least be safe, respectful, cooperative, and caring, regardless of whether they are close friends or not.

Schools cannot require kids to become true friends. They can however create the circumstances where student-to-student relationships are civil and kind and where true friendships are more likely to grow. The story of my son's teacher in Scotland seating him near boys she thought would be most likely to befriend him is a good example. One of the elements of increasing the likelihood of kids finding their kindred spirits is to foster healthy relationships between all kids, especially in the same classroom, in the context of shared norms about how we all want to be treated every day.

Hal Urban used the first three weeks of the school year in part to get each of his high school students to interview every other student and the teacher. They were asked to learn their names and five facts about each of them, an assignment that is described in his book *Lessons from the Classroom*. Many teachers use games that help students learn about each other and have fun together during the first week or two of the school year. Some play "two truths and a lie" where everyone writes two true facts about themselves plus one fact that is not true and the rest of the students have to guess which is which. Some have students write facts about themselves on a piece of paper (with no name on it). They crumple them up and have a silly "snowball fight." Then everyone picks one up at random, reads it aloud and has to guess who it is about. Others bring in baby pictures and they guess who is who. And so on. Remember, two keys to building relationships are to learn about each other and to have fun together. Most such "unity builders" incorporate both elements.

Another strategy is to periodically switch students' seats so they eventually sit next to everyone else in the class. Naturally, if you give students the choice of seating, they will choose to sit near their friends and away from people they either do not know or do not particularly like. Remember that we said the teachers with hearts for kids will help build relationships naturally, except for the kids who need it most. Allowing kids to choose whom they sit next to is a good example of that. Hal Urban allowed his students to do that but told them that it was temporary. He describes an elaborate but easy seat rotation system that he used. When students are seated at tables (of about four) these groupings should be rotated periodically. Often we think students will resist, and they may. But they also see the wisdom in it. At one school that was part of the Child Development Project, numerous students in a class of 11- and 12-year-olds suggested in a class meeting that this be done so they would get to know each other better (the video, called *Teasing*, is on our website: www.characterandcitizenship. org). These students were wise enough to understand the importance of relationships among all students in the classroom, particularly as a way to improve class climate and to reduce teasing.

While creating the initial steps of relationships is important, so are ongoing structures that increase the likelihood of deeper sustained relationships. I am a big fan of looping, that is, keeping the students together as a cohort, ideally with the same teacher, for more than one school year. An excellent variation is to create structures with mixed age/grade students. There are two predominant versions of this, one for elementary school and one for middle and high school (secondary school in many countries other than the US). In the US, elementary schools tend to have intact classes that exclusively or largely learn all subjects together, but middle schools and high schools more typically have students mixing each class period as they move to different subject teachers (in the US, teachers "own" the classroom and the students relocate whereas in many other countries the students "own" the room and the teachers relocate).

In US elementary schools, we sometimes see vertical structures. In a typical version of such a structure, two or three students from each grade level in the school plus an adult are part of a "family." The families ideally meet once a week. The activities vary widely but tend to include simple relationship building activities, cross-age curricular activities, and service activities. In most cases, the adult is a teacher, but at schools like Mark Twain Elementary in Brentwood MO (a NSOC), all adults in the school led a family. Besides the classroom teachers, Karen Smith the principal had one, but so did her secretary Marie, as did the cook and the custodian and the counselor and the librarian, etc.

Another variation of elementary school mixed age groupings is "buddying." In a perfect situation, an elementary school would have an even number of grade levels (for example, kindergarten through fifth grade is a common elementary school structure) and the same number of classrooms at each grade level, and the same number of students in the paired (buddying) classrooms. In this case, every kindergarten class would be paired with a third grade class, every first grade class with a fourth grade class and every second grade class with a fifth grade class. Then each student would be assigned a "buddy" in the matched classroom. Ideally, they would meet weekly, at first to simply do relationship-building activities, but then to do cross-grade curricular activities. A great resource for buddying is *That's My Buddy!* from the Center for the Collaborative Classroom.

At the secondary (middle school/high school) level, US schools sometimes have homeroom or advisory structures where students are assigned to a teacher for the year, ideally in smaller groupings than classroom size groups, to build relationships, do advising and counseling, and to serve as a home base with an adult who gets to know them better. When Bob Hassinger was Principal of Halifax Middle School in Pennsylvania, one of the first middle schools to be recognized as a National School of Character, he instituted multi-aged, looped advisories. There were about five or six students from each of the three grades in his school assigned to the same advisory. They also stayed together for all the years they were in the school with the same teacher. High schools can do the same with the typically four grade levels they have. In this way, students not only develop a sustained relationship with a teacher, but they also develop two- or three-year relationships with a few students from the grade above and the grade below them. As school climate and restorative practices consultant Jo Ann Freiberg notes, the mixed grade aspect also tends to reduce much of the negative hierarchical targeting that happens within grade levels. A caution is not to let this special time devolve into an academic study hall. Its power is in relationship building.

The largest set of student–student relationship-building strategies are peer interactive pedagogical strategies. These are instructional strategies that incorporate peer cooperation and collaboration. Most of these are familiar to most educators as curricular methods; however, because of their peer interactive structures they are also excellent character education methods. Nevertheless, in some cases there are clever ways to "turbocharge" the character development impact of the method. We will discuss how to do this for cooperative learning in the Developmental Pedagogy section.

There are plenty of other curricular methods that are peer interactive in nature and have the potential to nurture the development of character. Reading circles, peer tutoring, and group service learning are examples of ways to use peer interaction around academic curricula. Additionally, some of the peer relationship-building structures discussed earlier can also be integrated with academic learning. For example, elementary school vertical families and secondary school advisories can be used for academic purposes. As noted earlier, elementary school buddying can also be used for academic lessons.

Yet another set of strategies to promote student–student relationships has to do with directly enhancing the capacity to relate effectively with others and structures for both resolving interpersonal conflicts and repairing damaged relationships. The best resource for enhancing interpersonal competence comes from the field of social-emotional learning (SEL). The Collaborative for Academic, Social and Emotional Learning (CASEL; www.casel.org) offers a valuable website and corresponding resources to support the development of both intrapersonal and interpersonal competencies. The latter include competencies such as perspective-taking and empathy. Furthermore, SEL has many evidence-based curricula that focus on such competencies, many of which were included in the research reviews upon which PRIMED and this book are based. We will explore SEL more deeply in the Developmental Pedagogy section.

One unique and effective such program is Roots of Empathy (ROE), which was conceived and designed in Toronto by Mary Gordon. ROE pairs a new mother and infant with a trained ROE facilitator and brings them into elementary and middle school classrooms. There are lessons delivered while the students sit in a circle around the mother and infant and learn about feelings, communication, empathy, and other relational concepts.

Being proactive and preventive is the principal way to build character, but people and relationships do go awry. So reactive strategies are necessary too. When students find themselves in interpersonal conflicts, schools need ways to end the tension and help the students move forward. One way to do this is through peer conflict remediation programs, such as *Talk It Out* by Barbara Porro. We will return to this category of peer interactive strategies in the Intrinsic Motivation and Developmental Pedagogy sections.

There is a set of peer interactive pedagogical strategies that are designed specifically to enhance critical thinking about social and moral issues, called interpersonal and/or moral reasoning. Every person needs the capacity to critically and effectively reason about social challenges, including moral issues. Such capacities develop in large part from the practice of grappling, either alone or with others, with such problems, both real and hypothetical. Thus, a main strategy for teachers is to facilitate peer dilemma discussions whereby students collectively grapple with what are the best courses of action for protagonists in a dilemma. Sometimes the dilemmas are short written scenarios. Sometimes they are clips from movies (as is the case for Character Challenge, www.characterchallenge.org, and Film Clips, http://filmclipsonline.com/), but they may come from the curriculum or current events. Facilitating such discussions so that they are developmentally productive usually requires targeted professional development, however.

As should be obvious from this relatively brief and incomplete review, there are many ways to foster healthy relationships between students (and with teachers) in the school. Given the foundational importance of a healthy relational culture among teachers and students, schools would be remiss not to employ as many of these strategies as possible. Of course, the standard response is that there is not enough time in the day or, "There is too much on my plate." But as we have already noted, time is malleable, and we tend to allot it to what we Prioritize most. If our school-based values do not prioritize Relationships, then our values should be re-examined. Furthermore, a relational culture is not just good for character development but is also implicated in most reviews of best academic practices too.

• • • • •

Relations with and Among Other Stakeholders in the School

When one lists the stakeholder groups in a school, there are quite a few. We have already considered relationships between students and other students, teachers, and, to a small degree, administrators. In some systems, teachers are thought to include other professional staff like mental health professionals, but, in some cases, they are considered separate categories. Even teachers can be subdivided into classroom teachers and "special subject" teachers such as art, music, special education, and physical education. Administrators also are sometimes broken down into subgroups, as in Singapore where they routinely differentiate between Principals and middle management (department heads, instructional leaders, etc.). However you categorize teachers, administration and other professionals in the school, the one group that often gets missed are the "non-professional" or support staff (such as secretaries, cooks, custodians, teachers' aides, bus drivers, security guards, etc.).

First we will examine relationships between students and support staff and then turn to the critical issue of the adult culture of the school. In many schools, the support staff are invisible and anonymous. They have no formal mechanism for interacting with students. When they do, as in the cafeteria during lunch or driving them to and from school on school buses, they often complain that the students do not thank them, take them for granted, do not call them by name, ignore (even defy) their behavior management suggestions, etc. Nevertheless, in many schools the most charismatic and beloved adult is a custodian, cook, nurse, or secretary. These individuals seem to effortlessly and naturally leverage their genuine love for kids into relationships with many if not all the students. This raises the specter of the wasted potential for nurturing relationships between such staff and students. Healthy relationships, among any of these school stakeholder group members, are the building blocks of good schools and good character.

When I realized this fertile and neglected territory for building relationships and contributing to the overall climate of the school, I devised a simple strategy. Have every class/homeroom/advisory "adopt" an adult who does not already lead a class/homeroom/advisory. Of course, if you follow the suggestion earlier in the book, then every adult in the school would be leading an advisory or vertical family. If you do not do that, however, then this is an alternative. The adopted adult would be invited to the class, and the students would learn about him/her and s/he would meet the students. If you recall Kim McConnell's structure for a student interview of their new teacher, you can see how that could be adapted to students learning about their adopted staff member. Then the adoptee would be anointed an honorary member of the class and invited to join them whenever possible. Additional ideas are to invite them to special events (the class concert or play, a holiday party, etc.) and to throw them a surprise birthday party or in other ways honor them.

Perhaps the secret ingredient in building a school that optimally fosters the development of character does not even include any students in its focus or implementation. It is the adult culture. When Anthony Bryk and Barbara Schneider studied the adult culture in a large sample of Chicago schools, they uncovered this secret ingredient. What they found was a direct link between the culture of "relational trust" among the staff and the academic achievement of the students. In other words, the more the staff trusted each other and related to each other out of a culture of trust, the better their students learned. This is hard for many folks to accept. How could how teachers feel about each other raise test scores when so much time and energy and resources are expended on improving curricula and teaching methods and yet still are not enough to produce large gains in academic achievement?

One part of this puzzle is the fact that whole school climate has been linked strongly to student achievement—and to character development—of course. All too often, we forget that part of the whole school culture is the adult culture. Once, when I was a guest lecturer in a teacher preparation course, I asked these future teachers what they hoped to teach eventually. One student surprised me by not identifying a subject or grade level. He told me that he wanted to work in the high school he had attended. When I asked him why, he replied, "because I saw how well the teachers got along there and I would like to be part of that." A very wise student, but he is far from unique. As we shall see in the section on Modeling, students are very aware of teachers' behaviors, moods, attitudes, and relationships. How teachers get along does influence the students both directly and through the differing motivation of the teachers to do their jobs optimally.

Furthermore, if we use the analogy of corporate culture, it is very clear that the culture of an organization affects worker productivity, attendance, and even health of the staff. As a school experiences a positive adult culture, they will be more likely to like to come to work, to actually come to work, and to do better work/teaching.

Seeing the school as a complex social system helps. And understanding that in systems all the parts and relationships are intertwined and influence all the others. An excellent model in psychology for understanding this is Relational Developmental Systems, originally from Bill Overton and now championed by Rich Lerner at the Tufts

University Institute for the Advancement of Research on Youth Development. Essentially, RDS positions all development in the context of a complex set of systems, institutions, and most importantly relationships. Hence nurturing development means leveraging such relationships. It is not difficult from an RDS perspective to understand how adult relationships affect the adult culture, which influences the whole school culture and the development of students' character.

All too often we take the adult culture for granted, and that is a mistake. I ask the participants in my Leadership Academy in Character Education each year to survey their staff about the adult culture. They are often surprised, even stunned, to see rough spots that they did not know were undermining the school climate and success, both in academics and character development.

One of the critical elements in improving adult culture is leadership. Since we have already addressed leadership in the Prioritization section, here I will only make a few additional points. Intervening with adult culture to nurture, heal, and improve it is most centrally the job of the school administration. While I am admittedly biased, having been investing heavily in principal training for the past two decades, I would claim it is the main responsibility of the lead administrator. It is the leader's job to take care of the adult culture, and the teachers' job to take care of the kids. Sadly, we neither make this clear to school leaders nor do we prepare them for this critical leadership role. Recently, Keith Marty, the exemplary superintendent of the Parkway School District in St. Louis (a National District of Character), challenged me that the problem with educational leader preparation in the US is that we do not "prepare leaders to have difficult conversations with adults." Too many administrators do not shepherd the adult culture because they are afraid to confront or challenge staff or because they do not even know they should, and, if they do, they often do not know how to do it constructively.

Megan Tschannen-Moran has identified five characteristics of leaders who build trust in their staff. These "5 Facets of Trust" are mostly character strengths: Benevolence, honesty, openness, reliability, and competence. This is a recipe for principals to get others to trust them. We could easily add courage to that list.

Another group that we have already noted as routinely left out of discussions of school improvement are the support staff. We already discussed structures for building healthy student-support staff relationships, but we also need to consider the relationships between the educational professional staff and the support staff. These two groups are likely to know each other, as the custodians/cleaners clean the classrooms and respond to teacher requests for specific custodial needs. The secretaries often are the conduits to both getting clerical work completed and communicating with parents. However, teachers are far less likely to know the bus drivers, the cooks, and others. Even when they do know each other, it is easy to fall into a class structure between the "professional" and "non-professional" staff as they are frequently called, just as there is between administration and teachers, especially in cultures where such hierarchical divisions are prominent in the structure of the society or ethos of the school. This can put a limit on the depth of the relationships across such social groupings and hierarchies. Again, it is the leader's job to build a more egalitarian and inclusive adult culture.

One way to reduce the gap and build such relations has already been discussed, the classroom adoption of non-teaching adults. We talked about how this builds a relationship between the students in the classroom and the "adopted" staff. Importantly it also allows the teacher in the "adopting" classroom to build a relationship with the class adoptee.

It is also helpful for the school leader to model relationships with support staff. Empowering them as Karen Smith did by giving them the same roles and relationships with students as teaching staff models this. When Karen included her secretaries, cooks, and custodians in leading vertical families and mentoring at-risk children, she modeled for all her staff how to be inclusive of the support staff. A former dean of mine not only went way beyond the norm to support her administrative assistant in earning her college degree but, when the Dean moved to another state, she flew back to attend her former administrative assistant's graduation ceremony. This modeled for the entire faculty at our College of Education how to respect, serve, and develop an authentic caring relationship with support staff and scaffold their life journeys.

I am always impressed when I arrive at a school to provide professional development workshops and discover that *all* staff are present. When Stephanie Valleroy was principal of Northview High School (a special education high school in St. Louis and a NSOC), she sent all of her staff to earn character education certification through CharacterPlus, a St. Louis-based regional professional development organization. I teach part of the certification program. I was at first surprised and later simply pleased to meet the group from Northview at each workshop including a secretary, or teacher's aide, or custodian. Sitting at a table would be five to ten staff from Northview working together for the day on learning about best practices in character education and building deeper relationships while doing so. These strategies by great principals like Karen Smith and Stephanie Valleroy are also examples of Empowerment, the E in PRIMED.

Schools often have staff social events, and some are open to all staff, but often events and structures like these do not include the support staff. They should. When such events are open to the families of staff (such as a staff picnic), then the opportunity arises—not only for developing a relationship with the support staff—but also getting to know each other's families, which provides a different way to bond. Some of the great principals you have already met in this book routinely hosted staff family picnics at their homes and included *all* staff.

In the next chapter, we will turn to strategies for building relationships with school stakeholders who reside outside the formal structure of the school, that is, folks who are not students and who do not work at the school.

13

•••••

Relationships with External Stakeholders

A central theme of this section on relationships is the identification and inclusion of all stakeholder groups. The previous chapter addressed relationships within and between students, teachers, administrators, and support staff. That leaves two important stakeholder groups: (1) parents and other caretakers and (2) other external stakeholders. Stakeholders are those who have a vested interest in the school's impact. External stakeholders here refers to people who are not students nor school employees. Relating to parents is recognized as important, although often not fully developed, but other community members are more likely to be overlooked. First, we will discuss relationships with parents, then relationships with other external stakeholders.

•••••

Relationships with Parents

All relationships are more likely to develop and flourish when we learn about each other, spend positive time with each other, collaborate with each other, and share power with each other. This increases the likelihood of mutual respect and trust. So how can we do that with parents? In this case, I am mostly going to focus on the relationships between teachers and parents and not between parents and other school members such as support staff and administrators. The principles are the same, although the specific practices may differ.

Learning about each other sets the context for healthy relationships. We discussed one such strategy when we introduced the student interview of their new teacher. If you remember, when students wrote their teachers' biographies as homework, they were also required to get their parents to read them, ensuring that parents began to know the teacher. Some teachers provide more detail about themselves, sometimes by writing some autobiographical information that is shared with parents either in print or on a website. Others present themselves more fully when meeting parents, such as at open school night or in rarer cases when visiting the home. In a less systematic way, a teacher can be more or less self-disclosing in private conversations with parents, either in regular parent–teacher conferences or in special meetings to deal with special issues. Remember my son's K5 teacher who was excellent at relating to students but less comfortable relating to parents? She starred in teacher–student relationship building but struggled in what we are discussing here. As a teacher, are you willing to tell a parent that you have experienced the same struggles they are having or, that, as a child, you struggled with the same things their child is facing? Where appropriate, such self-disclosure can tear down social walls and nurture a deeper relationship.

Another interesting way to promote such relationships is by learning about the parents through a parent survey. Teachers, particularly in the elementary or primary grades, often send home a survey about the child for the parents to submit. One teacher also created a survey for the parents to fill in about themselves. For example, she asked about their experience, skills, and interests. This not only allowed her to have more personal interactions with the parents, but it also allowed her to increase parent involvement in her classroom, as we shall see shortly.

Beyond learning about each other, simply having positive interactions also supports relationship building. We will talk about the power of affirmation in the next section on Intrinsic Motivation, but it is helpful to mention here that when teachers call parents to tell them good news about their children ("I wanted you to know immediately how kind Kevin was today when he. . . ," "Guess what?! Ana got her first perfect grade on her math test today!" Etc.), they also help build a positive relationship with the parent. Of course, it is always a good relationship strategy to focus on the other person in positive ways, including simply asking about the other person, in this case the parent(s). Such questions could be generic ("Where did you go to school when you were in the third grade?") or person-specific ("I noticed on your parent survey that you love musical theater. Do you sing?").

Collaborating is another way to build relationships. One way to understand this more fully is to consider three different ways or levels of relating to parents. First is "parent as audience." This is very common. Schools should—and frequently do—inform parents of all sorts of things: Events, student progress, requests for contributions, etc. However, this implies a very one-directional and hierarchical relationship. Schools know. Parents need to know. Schools have information. Parents need information. There is nothing wrong with supplying information, but a real relationship has to go beyond an imbalanced unidirectional pairing.

The second type of relating to parents is "parent as client." Clearly, schools have expertise in a range of things and the physical resources to support them. They have experts, for instance, on health and on technology, and they usually have some health resources (such as a nurse's office) and technology resources (e.g., computers). Many parents need the resources that schools can provide. Therefore, opening the school (including at night and on weekdays after school hours) to parents for training and learning is a good way to support positive relationships with parents. Some schools formalize this by having a "parent university" where parents can come to learn about technology, health, or even parent specific issues like how to register to vote or fill out tax forms. Schools that have a large non-native English speaking population often offer something that is completely in the realm of expertise of every school, namely English language literacy education. Sometimes they merely open the school facilities for recreational purposes. The high school near my home when we lived in Shorewood Wisconsin and the school near our house when we lived in Scotland both opened up their swimming pools to the families in the community in the evening and on weekends.

However, just like for "parents as audience," "parents as clients" still is typically a one-directional hierarchical relationship. In this case, schools have expertise and resources; parents are in need of them. The third type of relation corrects this. It is best characterized as "parents as partners." A principal once came to me for advice on how to be more successful in engaging parents in his school. He told me that he had invited parents in as many ways as he could think of (letters home, website, emails, etc.) and then offered to feed them when they did come. However, they did not come. I pointed out that it was much like trying to get a pet dog to "come." "Here parents! Come parents! Want a treat?" He was a bit taken aback by my characterization of his strategy, but he got the point. Then I suggested he invite them in ways that were more egalitarian and respectful of who they were and what they bring to the table. We began this section by invoking the notion of collaboration. Here, at last, we are talking about true egalitarian collaboration, namely true partnership. Two good resources are the National Network of Partnership Schools at Johns Hopkins University and the National Association for Family, School and Community Engagement.

Status is often the undoing of teacher–parent relationships. Parents as clients or audience, as noted, implies a clear status difference. Many parents feel uncomfortable dealing with schools and educators and hence may resist working with schools and teachers. They may not feel competent to work with educators. They may not have had positive school experiences when they were students. They may be embarrassed of their literacy skills or lack of education. As a result, they may enter into such relationships with trepidation, or may avoid entering into them at all. The key point here is that schools need to be sensitive to how parents may experience them and then work to be more authentically invitational in ways that such parents can appreciate.

Another important aspect of relationship building is to treat others with respect. Parents often feel like the school sees them as a nuisance, a burden, or even an obstruction. Of course, some parents are. However, so are some educators! Moreover, some doctors and some secretaries and some clergy and some police and some social workers and. . . . In other words, people can be difficult sometimes, but to generalize and say all of a given group are problematic is distorted and counter-productive when trying to collaborate or merely work toward a common purpose. In fact, it is a good definition of prejudice.

Let us return to the teacher who surveyed parents about their interests, skills, and other characteristics. What she was able to do was reach out to them for specific forms of help and support that built on their strengths. Imagine being a relatively uneducated former factory worker who was injured and on disability income and who felt daunted about working with teachers, all of whom had bachelor's degrees, most of whom had master's degrees, and some of whom had doctoral degrees. Being invited to partner might feel threatening. Now imagine this teacher calling and saying, "Mr. Smith, I noticed on your survey that one of your hobbies is carpentry. I don't want to bother you, but we are planning on building a reading loft in our classroom, and I wondered if you could recommend a good place for us to buy supplies for building it." Not only will he feel respected to be asked for his advice, it is advice he feels confident and competent in providing. And my guess is that he will not only provide the requested advice but will actually come in and build it for you or, better yet, with you. Furthermore, he will forever be a willing partner and friend of the teacher and the entire class, which will be transformed in his mind from a threatening place where he does not feel he belongs to a place he finds comfortable, relevant, and appreciated. Build relationships by knowing others, treating them with respect, and authentically partnering with them. It is also important to note how this is not merely egalitarian but even shifts the status balance in favor of the parent. He becomes the expert, in fact the teacher, to the teacher. At Francis Howell Middle School, they created a school-wide database with information on parents so all teachers would know the special talents of all parents.

I had the opportunity to work with a team from San Guang Elementary School that serves a small indigenous Taiwanese peach farming mountain community in Fu-Xing Province. Because of the remote location, there are few if any qualified educators living near the school. So they contract with educators from cities hours away to work at the school. They live in housing specifically for this purpose. There is a natural divide between the adults in the community and the school staff. The staff members tend to remain at the school only for a couple of years. One significant problem was that, being largely subsistence farmers, the families could not afford to have their children in school during heavy farming labor seasons, such as harvesting. The kids frequently missed a lot of school. One year the principal, Eric Honglin Wu, came up with two brilliant ideas. First, rather than resisting the real family needs for the child labor, the staff began to help the community establish a commercial cooperative. Second, the students, using what they were learning in school about technology and writing, created a web page to market the peaches more widely. (By the way, these are some of the largest and most delicious peaches I have ever eaten.) The result? The farmers' income increased . . . tenfold. Moreover, the relationship between locals and school improved dramatically, with the farmers developing respect for the importance of schooling.

In our Leadership Academy in Character Education, we emphasize collaborative leadership. One way we do that is by having each participant form a school character education committee and, subsequently, doing all reflective assignments with them, meeting at least monthly to do that and other character education work. We also ask them to include representatives of all stakeholder groups, including parents, so they can be part of the collaborative work of designing, planning, implementing, and even assessing the character education initiative. In fact, we recommend that they add at least two parents (and support staff, etc.), so they can support each other. It is also a good idea to avoid the trap of including the same two parents as are included in many other school functions and structures (often the president and vice president of the parent teacher organization).

The former counselor at Lexington Elementary in the St. Louis Public Schools found a very creative role for parents. She asked parents, grandparents, and other guardians if they would be willing to video-record a minute or two simply stating what they hope their kids would be like. She then compiled them and made a video, which she used for behavior management. When a child was brought to her for disciplinary/behavioral reasons, she required them to watch the video of a set of parents and other guardians of the kids in this school describing their hopeful visions for kids. A great and unexpected side effect was that, in the eyes of the kids, the adults in the video were "movie stars." Many of these adults were not "stars" in any common understanding in our society, but kids would spot them in the parking lot picking up their kids and would exclaim with excitement, "You were in the movie!" Instant respect, and I would watch their faces light up for such recognition. This side benefit was yet another contribution to building school-to-home relationships.

Perhaps the most comprehensive and impressive form of school–parent relationships is community schooling. This starts with the recognition that a school is both community property and a great potential resource to the community. The Children's Aid Society's National Center for Community Schools (www.nccs.org) is a great resource for community schooling. Former Thomas Edison Elementary School (Yonkers, NY) Principal Eileen Santiago understood the value of such a perspective in her community of mostly lower socioeconomic Hispanic immigrant families. She also saw the natural fit between comprehensive character education and community schooling. Already a strong proponent of character education (Edison became a National School of Character under Santiago's leadership), they combined the Child Development Project with community schooling. Santiago made it clear to her community that they owned the school. She partnered with the parents to design how to best use the school to serve not only its student-focused missions (learning and development) but also its broader community, most notably the parents of her students. Her exemplary work is chronicled in her co-authored book, *Whole Child, Whole School*.

While these are some of the good ideas for how parents can have healthy and productive relationships with school staff, schools continually lament that parents simply do not engage with the school enough for such relationships to grow. Of course, this is a chicken-and-egg issue. What comes first, the relationship or parental involvement? They both come first, and they both come last. In other words, relationships make involvement more likely, and involvement makes relationships more likely. So just do both. Now we will turn to a specific model of increasing parent involvement.

There is a great model for understanding both what blocks parental engagement and what can be done to unblock it. Hoover-Dempsey and Sandler described four common obstacles to parental involvement. First, many parents may not know that they are supposed to be involved in their children's education. They may believe that children are the parents' responsibility at home and the educators' responsibility while at school, believing that teachers should not meddle in home life and parents should not meddle in school life. Research says the opposite, however. Appropriate constructive parent involvement in their children's education may be the single best predictor of student school success. Simply sharing such information with parents may get many of them to realize the power of their involvement in school. Another part of this first obstacle may be that parents, particularly those from marginalized and underserved communities and populations, may think their children cannot be successful at school. Research tells us that simply changing that parental "mindset" can get kids to reach higher levels of academic success. If such parents can come to believe their kids can succeed in school, then the kids are more likely to do so.

The second obstacle to parent involvement, one that was introduced earlier, is that parents may not feel competent to be involved with schools and/or educators. Finding roles for parents that are within their comfort levels is one good way to tackle this. We just described this in asking a parent to give carpentry advice as a result of using the parent interest survey. There should be many roles that most parents can do and would feel comfortable doing, such as chaperoning field trips. Moreover, there are roles that parents can fill due to their special talents, knowledge, and interests.

Many schools actually use the curriculum to help parents find ways they can competently contribute to their child's education. The Center for the Collaborative Classroom's *Homeside Activities* is a set of school-to-home-to-school academic activities. Children go home with an assignment that requires adult (ideally parental or guardian) involvement. It may be interviewing parents about something in the curriculum, teaching parents something they learned in school, or some other way to involve parents in curricular work. Ideally, the work then comes back to school and is used in the classroom for further learning. The topics can be directly about character; for example, one of the Child Development Project assignments is to interview a parent about the most courageous person they have known personally.

The third obstacle to parental involvement is that parents may not feel welcome in the school. Nowadays, in large part because of societal violence in general and school attacks in particular, many schools are more like fortresses than child-friendly community institutions. Simply getting into the school may be daunting (locked doors, armed guards, metal detectors, sign-in protocols), so many parents may shy away from going through what feels like an airport security system. There are many ways to make this safe and still friendly. When I visited the New City School in St. Louis, a great elementary school based on Howard Gardner's model of multiple intelligences, the door was unlocked. At the top of the entryway stairs was a desk, not staffed by an armed security guard but by a grandmotherly woman who immediately smiled and greeted me and asked me to sign in. I felt welcomed, not threatened. Chesterfield Elementary School in Missouri (a NSOC) has a lovely foyer with comfortable furniture for parents to use when waiting for a meeting or their child. Kennerly Elementary in

Missouri (another NSOC) used to have a video playing a charming loop of information and photos of kids for folks who were visiting the school.

Perhaps the most welcoming innovation was at a reasonably under-resourced inner-city elementary school where the first classroom inside the entrance had been converted to a parent resource center. There was a couch, tables and chairs, a coffee pot, and lots of relevant books and brochures for parents. There was a dedicated parent liaison. There were regularly scheduled events; for example, the nurse, counselor, and principal each had a designated half hour to be there each week either for presentations or just to talk or answer questions. There were special events, such as the counselor running a session on how children react to divorce and what parents can do about it or a teacher leading a discussion on how to help kids with homework when the parent does not know the material being studied. One can imagine that the parents at this school felt very welcome whenever they set foot in the school.

A fourth obstacle to parent involvement is that many parents feel unwelcome by their students. It is not a problem with the primary grades. Five-, six- and seven-year-olds would typically love it if their parents were there all day every day. However, as children get older they get less and less interested in hanging out with their parents. Middle school students typically not only do not want others to know you are their parents; they do not want others to know they even *have* parents. They would probably prefer people to think they were clones or test-tube babies. Therefore, schools may have to find ways to get kids to want their parents to be involved. In the section on the E in PRIMED (Empowerment), we will tell the story of a fifth grade teacher who used empowerment to get students to want their parents to see their classroom and to eagerly invite them to come to open school night.

Next, we will explore how to build relationships with and involve other external stakeholders.

● ● ● ● ●

Relationships with Other External Stakeholders

Perhaps the best way to ascertain who—or rather which groups of people—would most directly fall into the category of stakeholders external to the school staff, students, and parents is to ask yourself the question, "Who in the neighboring community would have a vested interest in the character of the school age youth in this community?" In other words, who should care about the effectiveness of your school in nurturing the flourishing of human goodness in the children and adolescents of this community?

If you really ask yourself who should care, you will likely identify many groups of relevance, such as nearby businesses, local government, firefighters, police, health-care workers, sanitation workers, retirees, etc. It is actually a great exercise for school personnel to brainstorm this topic, and it can lead them to see their work in a different, broader, and more impactful light and come to recognize the interconnectedness of the profession of education and the needs of the community. Character education is, after all, really about building a better world (*Tikkun Olum*), including locally.

Now we will examine some best practices in both building relationships and collaborating with external stakeholders. First, let us quickly review the fundamental principles of building relationships and collaborating authentically and effectively. To build relationships, we should listen to each other, learn about each other, have fun experiences together, and work together (ideally on something that is meaningful both in general and to both parties in particular). To authentically and effectively collaborate, we should communicate effectively, serve the other, empower the other, and work as equals. What are some examples of this?

Let us start with law enforcement. In the US at least, there is a common role for police to play in many schools. We often call it a "school resource officer" (SRO). This is a police officer who is assigned to a school to be present in the school and mainly engage in education, for example, about drug use or the law. Other roles the officer can play are in intervening with and at times advocating for students in the school who run afoul of the law or who are showing signs of becoming a juvenile offender. Clearly, another role is to provide police protection for and within the school. These roles can be effective in contributing to character education or can impede it. Much of that has to do with the R in PRIMED . . . relationships. If the SRO is able to relate to the students well, and they like and respect their SRO, then that opens the door for both effective implementation of the SRO's duties and character development of the students. If, on the other hand, students see the SRO as irrelevant, a threat, uninformed, or in other negative ways, then it can backfire.

A classic example is the DARE drug prevention program that has existed in many US schools for decades. Schools received it free. A DARE officer provides drug education at school. Schools love it because, for no cost, they receive a national drug prevention program, student exposure to a positive police presence in the school, and lots of cute trinkets (t-shirts, bumper stickers, etc.). Unfortunately, after decades of delivering this program, research clearly demonstrated not only that it did not reduce drug use, its primary purpose, but, in fact, for some groups it actually increased drug use. Despite this overwhelming research evidence of program ineffectiveness, schools and parents often vehemently protected the program and resisted replacing it with an effective drug prevention program, of which there are many. One actually said to me, "I don't care what the research says. I can make up my own research to show it works." Really.

Fortunately, DARE finally acknowledged the research and retooled the program. The jury is still out on whether the new program is effective.

An interesting aside to ponder is why it is almost unheard of for parents and community officials to worry that teaching about drugs would increase its use, while they frequently worry about whether sex education should be allowed in schools, because they think teaching about sex will increase sexual activity, which research suggests it does not do.

We often recommend inviting a local law enforcement official such as the local chief of police to serve on the school's character education committee. This strategy applies as well to every other category of external stakeholders that we will discuss or that you can think of. If you establish a school character education leadership team/ committee, think about all the external stakeholder groups who could be included as members of the team/committee.

Another cross-cutting strategy for all external stakeholder groups is to formally thank and honor them. Schools do this in many ways. When Janis Wiley was principal of Mann Accelerated School in the St. Louis Public Schools, she was in a diverse and vibrant community with many "neighbors," many of whom interacted with the school. Once a year her elementary school organized a breakfast for local "friends." This included the many different ethnic restaurants nearby, the administrators of the large park near the school, the administrators of the Botanical Garden in the neighborhood, local law enforcement, etc. The elementary school students served the meal, created the placemats and table decorations, provided entertainment, and thanked their neighbors for being their friends. There were no strings attached, no "ask." They simply expressed their gratitude and thereby enhanced relationships with external stakeholders/neighbors.

When Brian O'Connor was Principal of Nottingham Career and Job Training School in the St. Louis Public Schools, a special education high school for most developmentally delayed students, the neighbors were uncomfortable with these "odd" kids who were now in their community every day in what had been a neighborhood middle school. The students were being taught job and career skills, such as gardening and custodial work, services that some members of the local neighborhood needed. O'Connor found opportunities for the students to serve their neighbors, for example by gardening services, which built a bridge over the former chasm of discomfort and distrust.

These two examples are nice segues to looking at relationship building and collaboration with local businesses. One of my favorite examples comes from Kennesaw Mountain High School in Georgia. Just as for relating to and collaborating with parents, all too often relationships with other external stakeholders tend to be one-dimensional and/or hierarchical. The most common such relation is to simply ask the broader community to support the school's character education initiative, typically through financial donations. While it is fine to do this, it tends not to build meaningful relationships. Here is what Kennesaw Mountain did. They created a character education structure, which was a monthly morning gathering. Every student attended once during the year. They started a bit before the normal school start and served breakfast. Then, incorporating the first class period of the day, they held a character education assembly including a high-profile speaker about a character topic. When the speaker was done, the students were grouped into small discussion groups proctored by the teachers who normally would have been teaching them during that class period. But they added a brilliant addendum. They approached local businesses and said something like, "Hi. We are from Kennesaw Mountain High School and wonder if you would support our character education program." When the businessperson, probably unenthusiastically and resignedly, asked, "How much do you want?" the response surprised them. They discovered that they were not being asked for funding but rather to allow a couple of their employees to come to the high school one morning per month to have breakfast with the students, hear the lecture, and then *co-facilitate* a discussion of a character topic. This was not a big ask. It likely entailed two hours per month during the school year, slightly over two workdays for each participant over the course of the entire year. Furthermore, from the point of view of the volunteers, this looked quite attractive. Get singled out to get out of work and still be paid for two hours per month, get a free breakfast, hear a charismatic speaker about character, and then help lead what were likely rip-roaring discussions of ethical issues with engaged high school students.

The secret ingredients in this example are respect and partnership. They respected the businesses and their employees. Moreover, the volunteers were full partners in leading the discussions. It ended up with a surprising side benefit. Because of the way they treated their community stakeholders, they started getting unsolicited offers of support from some of the businesses who were sending employees to the school, something they might not have gotten even by directly asking for it. A meaningful relationship had been built, one that likely would endure because it was authentic and born of respect and partnership.

Another business stakeholder example comes from the Hamilton County (TN) Public Schools. A character education initiative that started in the countywide school district surrounding Chattanooga was wisely expanded to incorporate a broad range of external stakeholder groups. This project is chronicled in a book entitled *A Gift of Character: The Chattanooga Story* by Vincent, Reed, and Register. Once the schools had settled on a set of monthly character words, they asked their community partners to join in reinforcing them. Business owners were asked to post the word of the month in their businesses and talk to students about them. Some businesses invested more heavily. The local paper published a monthly section on character focusing on the word of the month. A billboard company donated billboards highlighting the word of the month.

Many other stakeholder groups also participated. One of the more interesting ones is local clergy. They were brought together and asked how they could be involved. Many began to explicitly incorporate the character words into their sermons and other messages to their congregations.

Many communities have local civic organizations or chapters of national and international civic organizations (for example, Masons, Kiwanis, Lions Club, etc.), which are looking for worthwhile projects to support both financially and by volunteering. Many schools and districts build partnerships with them. In some cases, these organizations have a national or international commitment to a specific character education program that they underwrite.

While there are many more examples of external stakeholders, the last group we will discuss here may be surprising, at least in considering it "external." That is other schools. There are many ways a school can build a relationship with or collaborate with other schools, both within their own district or external to it, either in general or specifically to support character development.

A common example is for students from older grade schools to work with students in younger grade schools within the same district. This can be for curricular and/or developmental purposes. It has most typically been done as leadership training or as a service activity for the older students. It tends to be very hierarchical. We already learned about one of my favorite examples; that is, the case of an elementary school in South Carolina where students learned about elections and went to a neighboring high school to find eligible students who were not registered and offered to help them register to vote.

Earlier we talked about the value of multi-aged looped middle and high school advisory/homeroom classes. I have recommended that schools that can identify their incoming next year's class (for example the current elementary school graduating fifth graders who will be the incoming sixth graders in the middle school the following school year) build a relationship with their feeder schools in order to build relationships between the future sixth graders and the homeroom/advisory to which they will be assigned when they move up to the secondary school. A yearlong process of relationship building can happen before the student ever moves to the next school. Knowing how treacherous school transitions can be, especially for adolescents, this is a great way to make that transition smoother and less traumatic. It is worth noting that transitions are often most toxic for students of trauma, and considering ways to lessen the added trauma of all school transitions would be highly advisable to support them toward success in school.

Many programs try to strategically build relationships between schools that have very different student populations. EnTeam, a wonderful program that aims to build peace and character through promoting cooperation, mainly through creating structures whereby cooperation can be measured and success tracked in the effectiveness of cooperation, often applies its social, academic, and sports cooperative structures to bring together schools with very different populations. Ted Wohlfarth, EnTeam's founder, has done this with racially and socioeconomically disparate schools and ethnically and religiously disparate schools (for example, a Muslim, a Christian, and a Jewish school). Students engage in cooperative games and structures within heterogeneous groupings both to learn cooperation and to learn about each other and to build healthy relationships across societal barriers.

I earlier emphasized the wisdom in investing in your feeder schools, that is, the schools that their students come from. If we did not believe our schools could make a difference in who students are, what they know, and how they act, then why are we even talking about character education—or education at all, for that matter? High school teachers, for example, should routinely help their middle school colleagues, mentoring them, helping them access academic resources, sending their own students as tutors, etc.

We have now explored the very complex world of relationships. We have seen how critical they are to school success and character formation. We have seen how they are activated by certain key elements like authenticity, listening, power sharing and balances, etc. We have seen levels of cooperation and advocated for authentic partnerships as most transformative. Furthermore, we have explored a very wide range of relationships both within the school and beyond it. Moreover, we have offered a set of evidence-based concrete examples and practices, with the understanding that this is simply a sampling, and educators are creative and smart and will generate many more. In fact, almost all the examples in this book come from educators who have created them.

In the next section we turn to the third letter in PRIMED, the I, which represents Intrinsic Motivation. This may be one of the most contentious ideas in PRIMED, so buckle up and read on. But perhaps only after you have tackled the relationship worksheet following.

● ● ● ● ●

Resources for Relationships

Books

Berkowitz, M.W. (2012). *You Can't Teach Through a Rat: And Other Epiphanies for Educators.* Boone, NC: Character Development Group.

Dalton, J., & Watson, M. (2001). *Among Friends: Classrooms Where Caring and Learning Prevail.* Oakland, CA: Center for the Collaborative Classroom.

Developmental Studies Center (1995). *Homeside Activities: Conversations and Activities That Bring Parents into Children's Schoolside Learning.* Oakland, CA: Center for the Collaborative Classroom.

Developmental Studies Center (1997). *Blueprints for a Collaborative Classroom.* Oakland, CA: Center for the Collaborative Classroom.

Developmental Studies Center (1998). *That's My Buddy! Friendship and Learning Across the Grades.* Oakland, CA: Center for the Collaborative Classroom.

Santiago, E., Ferrara, J., & Quinn, J. (2012). *Whole Child, Whole School: Applying Theory to Practice in a Community School.* New York: Rowan and Littlefield.

Urban, Hal (2008). *Lessons from the Classroom: 20 Things Good Teachers Do.* Redwood City, CA: Great Lessons Press.

Vincent, P.F., Reed, N., & Register, J. (2001). *A Gift of Character: The Chattanooga Story.* Chapel Hill, NC: The Character Development Group.

Watson, M. (2019). *Learning to Trust: Attachment Theory and Classroom Management* (2nd Edition). New York: Oxford University Press.

Websites

www.casel.org
www.characterchallenge.org
www.collaborativeclassroom.org
www.enteam.org
http://filmclipsonline.com

www.nafsce.org
www.nnps.jhucsos.com
www.nccs.org
www.rootsofempathy.org
www.search-institute.org

PRIMED Action Planning Worksheet:

Relationship Strategies

Relationships: Intentionally developed positive connections between members of the school/district community. This includes all stakeholder groups. These relationships are based typically on positive interactions and shared knowledge of each other.

Evidence-based implementation strategies:

Within school:	Peer interactive pedagogical methods
	Intentional promotion of relationships
	Peer conflict resolution program
	Nurturing adults
	Teaching relationship skills
Beyond the school:	Relationships with families and/or community

STEP ONE:

Please identify at least two relationship-building strategies that are already in place in your school/district. You may use the previous categories or anything else you do that you think intentionally supports the development of healthy relationships.

1.

2.

3.

4.

STEP TWO:

Please identify at least two more things you can do that would increase the development of positive relationships in your school/district. Again, you can choose from the previous list or list anything else you think would be good for you to implement for the purpose of increased positive relationship development.

1.

2.

3.

4.

PRIMED Principle 3: Intrinsic Motivation (Internalization)

14

•••••

The What and Why of Intrinsic Motivation

We started this book by reflecting on purpose, the purpose of this book. We also touched upon purpose when we explored the P in PRIMED, namely Prioritization. Our fundamental purposes, by definition, should be our priorities. For this book, character education is the priority, the purpose of what we do and what we are trying to help you to understand, want to do, and be competent to do. But what does that purpose, that priority, mean for the individual student? What is the purpose of character education for that student? Hal Urban, author of *Lessons from the Classroom*, defines character as "bringing out the best in children." Another spin on this is nurturing the best *in* the child. It is the preposition "in" that is the doorway into understanding Intrinsic Motivation.

Another common definition of character is what you do when no one is watching. You do it because you are it. It is in you. It is you. When my son was struggling in his early twenties, he decided that he should move to another city and start over. He reasoned that relocating would be wiping the slate clean from his recently misdirected life. I said, "That's an interesting idea. However there is one problem with it." When he asked what I meant, I continued, "Unfortunately, wherever you go you are going to have to take you with you." To his credit he replied, "Good point." The point is that our character resides within us, and that if we want to change character, we have to target that which is within us. If character is what you do when no one is watching, then how can that "no one" reward or praise you? It must be done for intrinsic, internal reasons and not for external rewards or recognition. Otherwise, no one would do the right thing when nobody is watching.

We have also talked about character education as fundamentally a *way of being*. We should look at character itself in the same way. Your character is your way of being. It is more than simply what you think or what you actually do. From the point of virtue theory, a virtue is an integrated part of the person that connects values, actions, emotions, and thoughts into a way of being that is virtuous. To be compassionate is to prioritize (value) compassion, to understand it, to feel the relevant emotions (empathy, sympathy, etc.), and to act in ways that are compassionate based on those values and feelings and under the guidance of good reasoning about how to be compassionate in a particular instance. This is clearly a characteristic of the person—and a complex one at that.

If character is one's central way of being, this should naturally lead to the question of why a particular person has a particular way of being. That question is about the source of character in a person. I have asked people all over the world that question, and the most common answers are about relationships (the R in PRIMED) and role models (the M). Others talk about the traumas and hurdles they had to overcome in life. No one has ever claimed that their character came from extrinsic rewards or public recognitions.

One way to think about this is through the motivation one might have to be a person of character or to be a person with a particular character strength or virtue. The answer is a response to the question: Why be good? Psychologists would look at this as a question of motivation or what Daniel Pink calls "drive." What motivates you to *be* a certain way rather than some other way? What motivates you to be honest, compassionate, responsible, or courageous—or the opposite?

The point here is that whatever you call this motivation, ideally, it is something inside of you rather than something external to you. This gets us closer to understanding the I in PRIMED.

While the I in PRIMED stands for Intrinsic Motivation, it could also stand for internalization. By this I mean the relocation of values from the parents, teachers, school, and community (*outside* the child) to residing *inside* the child. Getting those values to shift from being the values proposed, advocated, and even modeled by others to being values that the child holds herself . . . within herself. We want those values to move from being something we know, understand, and see to something we are. That is internalization. When values are ours, inside us, and held dearly by us, they become our motivation. We are motivated to follow those values because we are those values, because those values are part of who we are. That is the nature of Intrinsic Motivation.

If we truly want to engage in effective character education, then we need to figure out how to get kids to internalize what we teach and model. This section of the book will explore what research tells us works in fostering the internalization of values and promoting the Intrinsic Motivation to adhere to them in our words and our deeds, so that we truly and fully become people of character, and so we do not merely act a certain way in the moment.

While it is overly simplistic to talk about motivation as either extrinsic or intrinsic, it is helpful to start with this dichotomy. Let us think of a child who is trying to decide whether to tell the truth about something uncomfortable (e.g., a close friend's transgression) or who is trying to decide whether to be courageous and confront a bully who is targeting another child. The motive to be honest or courageous could come from within or from outside the child. Perhaps the child considers what he or she might gain (such as a reward or public acclaim) for doing so. That would be an external source or extrinsic motivator. Alternatively, the child might think about the kind of person she wants to be (honest or courageous) or simply what she values in life (truth, courage). Those would be internal to the child or intrinsic motives.

As educators, we should want our efforts to lead children to develop internal motives to be a person of character, so that wherever they go in life, they will take those motives, those character strengths, those virtues with them, rather than merely enacting them when the circumstances provide a motive external to themselves, such as when there are clear material rewards for being that way or when an authority is watching.

This may seem a vague and not very helpful goal, but, in fact, it is critical to the design and implementation of schools and any other attempt to influence child development for that matter. I often ponder what I call "the implicit theory of the child." I learned about this way of thinking about children and development from my undergraduate developmental psychology professor, Bill Overton. He offered three conceptions of children from the three predominant psychological theories of the day: Behaviorism; psychoanalytic theory; cognitive-developmental theory. Behaviorism contends that children are like all other animals and are motivated by external factors such as rewards and punishment, by the consequences of their actions. Psychoanalytic theory contends that children are a battleground upon which the warring factions of reason, conscience, and primal desires contend for dominance over the developing personality. Cognitive-developmental theory sees children as rational, self-directed, and intrinsically trying to make meaning of the world in which they exist.

The key point for us is that these theories then lead to different prescriptions about how to get kids to become good people. Behaviorism emphasizes rewards and punishments and external control to shape the children. It does not recognize even the possibility of other kinds of motivation within the child. Psychoanalysis favors promoting control over one's selfish and antisocial tendencies, sometimes by authority and sometimes by insight into one's unconscious forces and motives to gain some mastery over the selfish and aggressive ones and to allow the moral side of personality to gain ascendance. Cognitive-developmentalism suggests that children should be guided through exploration of the physical, social, and intrapsychic worlds and allowed to grapple with challenges and problems so they can co-author their developmental journeys. Very different approaches.

Well, what does this have to do with schools in general and with character education in particular? A lot, in fact.

Typically and unintentionally, educators tend to skew toward a behaviorist approach to helping kids become people of character. After all, shiny sparkly things attract us. Giving kids things that make them smile helps us feel good, and hence we feel justified in doing so. In fact, what happens is an educator uses extrinsic motivators (like stickers, candy, etc.), and they themselves are rewarded for doing so by the positive affect expressed by the child. It is essentially a double whammy effect. They use extrinsic motivators and are reinforced for doing so, which is both reinforcing the behaviorist strategy and behaviorist theory. Consequently, they do it even more.

All of this would be wonderful . . . if extrinsic motivators led to the internalization of values. Unfortunately, they do not. In fact, they tend to reduce the internalization of values, which means educators are using methods that actually undermine their fundamental goal, namely nurturing the flourishing of goodness *in* students. Next, we will explore the disadvantages of using extrinsic motivators in school, particularly for character education. Then we will turn to intrinsic alternatives that schools can and should use instead.

15

•••••

The Perils of Extrinsic Motivators

If you are an educator and a parent, it is a helpful thought experiment to consider the following questions. If you are a teacher but not a parent, imagine the role of the parent with your students at home. First, we will assume that parents want their own children to develop good character. If not I doubt you would be reading this book. Nearly all parents want their children to grow up and become good people; that is, they want to nurture the flourishing of human goodness in their children. So ask yourself the following questions about your parenting techniques designed to foster character development in your children:

• Do you spend your hard-earned money on posters with just a single word on them (e.g., respect, responsibility, honesty, integrity) and plaster them around your house?
• Do you rename the spaces in your house after character words, often with cute street signs; e.g., Karing Kitchen, Benevolent Bathroom)?
• Do you keep a ready supply of little pieces of paper, optimally shaped like an animal's footprint, in your pocket to give to your child when she does something nice?
• Do you have a supply of treats and rewards that they get when they amass enough of those slips of paper?
• Do you read your family a pithy quote about character to start every day (preferably through a system of speakers in your house)?
• Do you convene your family once per month to announce which member of the family had the best character that month?

Probably not. Then ask yourself the following question: If, as educators, you believe those strategies are so powerful and effective, why don't you use them with your own children?

Well if you are honest with yourself, then you will probably answer that question by recognizing that they are NOT that powerful. Yet educators turn to them constantly and staunchly resist replacing them with more effective strategies. I hope that you will be open to seriously considering and confronting the all-too-prevalent educator addiction to extrinsic motivators. One way to convince you is to take a closer look at what actually results from such extrinsic motivation.

The two most condemning outcomes of a method to foster character development would be (1) ineffectiveness (no impact on character) or (2) undermining (promoting bad character). Sadly, both are true of extrinsic motivators.

Perhaps the best source of such information is the research on Self-determination Theory (www.selfdeterminationtheory.org). Well over a quarter century of high-quality research by Ed Deci and Richard Ryan reveals that the worst kind of motivators are material rewards (things, even as simple as a sticker) that one knows in advance will be earned by engaging in certain behaviors. Unfortunately, schools do this routinely. Students know that if they show respect, act responsibly, or tell the truth, they will get a thing for it. I am told story after story of students "performing" acts of character on purpose in the presence of an adult simply to get the anticipated reward that everyone knows will follow such an act. One former superintendent in Canada tells of visiting a school and being greeted by a student who said, "Oh Miss, you look lovely today." When she graciously and sincerely thanked him, he kept following her. Then he repeated, more emphatically this second time, "Miss, you look lovely today." Somewhat quizzically, she thanked him again, to which he replied, "Where is my reward?" A principal told me the story of two middle school girls in the hallway whispering to each other as the principal and a teacher approached. One whispered to her friend, "Now. Do it now." The second dropped her books and the first immediately helped her pick them up—while looking at the principal—and then asked, "Do I get a Tiger Paw?"

Research shows that the use of a priori (they know in advance), contingent (you get the reward for doing something), and material (you get a thing) rewards reduces the internalization of respect, responsibility, honesty, or whatever aspect of character is being rewarded. It actually undermines the purpose of character education, which is the internalization of character . . . becoming a person of character rather than acting as if you are a person of character just for the anticipated reward.

There is study after study showing this effect. For example, toddlers become less altruistic when they are given a reward for being nice or helping. Adults become less compliant with their health regimens (for example, taking medication responsibly, dieting for health reasons, exercise for physical therapy) when they started being rewarded for doing so. In fact, schools tell us repeatedly how having a reward system for character not only diminishes prosocial behavior but actually increases misbehavior. As one experienced principal told me, "When we started using PBIS in our school, it turned the PBIS pyramid upside down. Instead of only 15% of kids misbehaving repeatedly, now the bottom 85% of the pyramid was on top and misbehaving repeatedly." She reported that she had to very slowly get the adults to accept this and wean themselves off their addiction to extrinsic motivators . . . and it was not easy. It really is not the kids who care about such rewards and recognitions; rather it is the adults (parents and school staff). They are looking where the light is, rather than where the keys are.

A very telling example was an elementary school in the Kansas City Public School district. They wanted to instill an ethic of service in their students, all of whom came from underserved disadvantaged families and communities. They designed a yearlong project to increase service among their students. It seemed to work, as students were logging more and more voluntary service activities. Then near the end of the school year, the school custodian announced that he was retiring after 30 years at the school. He was the most beloved adult in the school, essentially because he loved every kid and they all knew it. The teachers suggested to the kids that this was the perfect capstone for a year of service. They suggested the kids organize a surprise retirement party for the custodian. Surprisingly, they completely dropped the ball and never did it. When I asked if they knew why, they replied,

> Yes, we finally realized the problem. We had increased service by giving rewards for service. The kids increased service behavior but never internalized the value of service. They were just doing it for the rewards. There was no reward attached to the retirement party.

Extrinsic motivators may change behavior, but (1) the effects are ephemeral and go away when there are no rewards in play and (2) the treasured values are never internalized to become character, which is the whole point of this.

What we want is for the students to internalize the emphasized character strengths. When Jennifer Dieken-Buchek's class of nine-year-old students was given the school's "Golden Spoon" award (which came with an ice cream celebration party) by their principal for good behavior in the lunchroom, one student boldly stood up and addressed the principal. Knowing he was speaking for the class, he very respectfully said, "Thank you, but we don't want the ice cream party." When the stunned principal asked why, the student replied, "We should do it because it is the right thing to do, not for a reward." They had not only internalized the value of responsible lunchtime behavior, but, thanks to Jennifer, had also learned the principle underlying character development.

One high school I worked with had created a reward system for character. They had six core values, and each was color coded (red for respect, blue for responsibility, etc.). If you were "caught in the act" of being respectful, for example, you were given a red plastic bracelet. At the end of the year, all students who had the full set of six colored bracelets were entered into a drawing for a substantial prize. I asked the students if they liked this extrinsic system and the plastic bracelets. They answered, "Yeah, in fact we steal them from each other!" Get it? It was designed to promote moral character and instead it was breeding theft. Eventually, the principal had to pull the plug on the project because an entire black market had evolved simply to acquire the bracelets to get a chance at the prize. Students were actually stealing the bracelets and selling them to each other.

Kids will also see through the artificiality that often permeates such extrinsic motivational practices. My nephew, Hunter, once was named the "Character Kid of the Week" in his primary grade classroom. His mother, my sister Gail, was appropriately thrilled. When she wisely asked him what he had done to earn this recognition, his blasé reply was, "It was my turn."

I have heard many educators argue for what I call the "weaning theory." Recently a principal of a private school that focuses on special needs students made this argument to me. It goes like this. "With our student population, we need to first get them focused on trying to be good, so we have to start with extrinsic motivators. But then we wean them off of the rewards." It is a nice theory. However, in practice, it appears that the extrinsic motivational system is addictive to adults. When I asked that same principal if she actually does wean the kids off the rewards, she visibly blanched at the sudden realization that in fact they never do. This is sadly very common.

Another version of this is with the little ones, the preschoolers and kindergarteners. The argument is parallel. "At this age, they are developmentally focused on extrinsic consequences, so we have to use that. This is how they think the world works and this is how they decide what is right and wrong." That is an accurate description of children in the first five to six years of life. However, part of this argument is that we will then wean them off the rewards. Again, they simply do not do it. Extrinsics become the currency of the realm in preschool and primary grades . . . and beyond. Furthermore, we do not want simply to pander to developmental levels. Rather we want to help kids come to understand and navigate the world in more mature ways. In other words, we want to be developmental guides, assisting them in making developmental progress, in this case, to moving beyond rewards as a basis for doing and knowing the good. In the section on Developmental Pedagogy, we will explore this perspective more fully.

It is important to say something about punishment. Punishment is not an effective behavior change mechanism. It may stop a behavior immediately, but it is a poor developmental strategy. As a wise school counselor once told the teachers in her school,

When you punish a child for misbehaving in your classroom, and she stops, you think you have succeeded in reducing her misbehavior. Wrong. She will end up in my office later for doing something more serious, and often more than once, when you are not watching. You are breeding misbehavior, not stopping it, when you use punishment.

Parents who use extreme physical punishment are more likely to have children who become chronically violent. After all, we know that kids learn more from what we do than from what we say (more on this in the next section on Modeling). In addition, it tends to harm the relationships we talked about as fundamental in the prior section. As we will see in the next chapter, this is also a problem because punishments are usually unrelated to the misbehavior.

Many educators wisely eschew material rewards (and punishments) for social praise. This is a good move and something we will examine further in the next chapter. However, there are many ways to structure praise and, if done wrong, it can produce collateral damage. The most treacherous part of the social praise domain is the audience. Whether one is engaging in negative feedback (reprimand) or positive feedback (praise), having an audience opens the door for collateral damage. When I ask people to tell me the story of the worst teacher they ever had, the most common narrative is about public humiliation. One senior teacher told of a put-down in front of the class when she was in first grade. It was five seconds and was a sadly typical throwaway comment, the sort that belittles a child for her body shape or appearance, race, gender, religion, family background, etc. The teacher who made the disparaging hurtful comment probably did not remember saying it a half hour later. However, when this teacher tried to tell our study group the story, she could not finish because of the pain of the memory. She started to sob. She was 57. This had happened half a century earlier, and the emotional effects still throbbed.

Try never to have an audience when you reprimand a child. An audience is also treacherous for praise, but for very different reasons. One of the most common character education strategies is public recognition for character-related behavior. This can take many forms, such as whole-school character education assemblies, the character section of award assemblies, public address announcements of people of character excellence or acts of character, classroom announcements of the current "kids of character," etc. All share the same basic idea: Publicly identify models of character to influence the development of character in "the audience." However, here is where I get confused. What exactly is the theory about how these public affirmations actually accomplish the goal of fostering the flourishing of human goodness? I have tried to figure out what educators think happens. Here is what I assume that they think.

Susie Smith is publicly recognized as a kid demonstrating exemplary respect. Let us say this happens in a school-wide event. The assumption must be that the students sitting in the audience hear this announcement and think,

> Wow. Susie Smith is such a great role model for me. Because of her behavior and this public recognition, I am going to rededicate my life to becoming more respectful . . . and aspire to become more like Susie!

Really? Do you actually think kids think like that? Here is what probably really happens.

There may be a few who feel that way. Susie's best friends. More likely, they just think it is cool that one of them is getting her moment of fame and are probably not very focused on the "why." A few kids. Most of the rest of the kids are bored and wishing they were allowed to have and use their smartphones in such gatherings. Then there are the kids who are becoming very angry. "Susie Smith?!?!? Respectful? Don't they know what she says about her teachers behind their backs? She teases me relentlessly every day on the school bus. I hate this school!" Or, "Susie Smith?!?!?! She comes to school and acts respectfully once. I try to be respectful every day and no one even notices it. I hate this school!"

So far, this grand pedagogical practice has bored most of the students and alienated a bunch of others. Not much character development happening there. However, there is more. The next morning the school office phone tends to be ringing more often than usual, as parents call in to complain. "Why did Susie Smith get a character reward and my kid didn't? She came home in tears." Or, "Susie Smith? Really? I know that family and they are a bunch of losers. My kids never get recognized." Oops, more enemies and alienated school stakeholders.

Let us now tally up the score. A few pleased students (the ones getting the recognition and their few close friends). Lots of bored students. A group of disenfranchised alienated students. And a bunch of angry parents. Nice pedagogical choice, eh? All collateral damage from a well-intended, entrenched, and loved practice, albeit one that fails to deliver the internalization of character and actually is counterproductive by boring, alienating, and angering so many school stakeholders. Yet schools hang on to this practice as if their lives depended on it.

By the way, if that did not convince you, and you are an educator, think about this. If your school or district has a "teacher of the year" or similar designation, think about the reactions of the staff to each year's announcement of the selected staff member. Teachers repeatedly tell me that the same thing happens, only with more bitterness and alienation. "This is such a popularity contest. No way she is a better teacher than me." "How do those who vote even know how good a teacher anyone else is, anyhow?" Etc. More rancor, not much positive to contribute to improving teaching. More collateral damage.

We have seen that our goal is the internalization of positive values so they become who we are (even when no one is watching). Therefore, we become intrinsically motivated to be people of character, people who respect others, act responsibly, tell the truth, are fair and just, and can care about the well-being of others (even those who are different from us). Moreover, we have seen that using extrinsic motivators can actually undermine this goal and that public affirmation is ineffective and has lots of collateral damage. This is what Alfie Kohn meant when he titled his book on this topic *Punished by Rewards*.

As an important cautionary tale, I was told the following anecdote, although I know many more like it. A few years ago, a principal of a large elementary school reported that she had a very punitive kindergarten team. The teachers were using a common behavioral management technique of publicly and graphically representing each child's behavior during the day from good to cautionary to bad, represented as green, yellow, and red traffic lights respectively. They were routinely sending home the "traffic light" charts that sit on each student's desk. During one week, two children whose behavior had led to "non-green" lights brought these charts home. When this came home, the children were beaten, government child protective authorities had to be called, and the children were removed from their homes. That same principal shared that by the end of the same month, five more children had the same experience. In other cases, children are punished in other ways such as losing privileges, often just by parents who are trying to support school policies and practices. It is not surprising that such children begin showing gross school avoidance. As Jo Ann Freiberg argues, is not just that behavioral programs like PBIS and Classroom Dojo are based on faulty theory, it is doing real damage.

What should you do instead? What actually works to foster the flourishing of human goodness and to internalize those core values of the school? That, in fact, is what we explore in the next chapter.

16

•••••

Outside In: Designing Schools for Intrinsic Motivation

In this chapter, we will accomplish three things. First, we will identify two foundational elements that support the internalization of characteristics of human goodness. Then we will describe three broad shifts that we need to make in our schools to
increase the internalization of our selected character strengths, values, and virtues.
Then we will look at the specific evidence-based strategies for implementing effective
means of promoting Intrinsic Motivation.

•••••

Two Foundational Elements

We start (in theory) with the selected, emphasized values outside the child. They are
in the school, in its mission statement, on its walls, and in its rhetoric. The goal is for
them to migrate to within the character of the student. What would need to be in place
for this to be likely to happen?

First students need to feel *a sense of belonging* to the school and of emotional attachment to the adults in the school. Remember that belonging is one of the three fundamental motives identified and targeted by Self-determination Theory. Moreover, we
have done a deep analysis of the importance of relationships as one of the Six Design
Principles of PRIMED. Belonging is one face of Relationships.

Once students have an authentic sense of connectedness and belonging to the
school or to its subunits (such as the classroom, middle school team, or grade level)
and corresponding healthy relationships with the adults in the school, then they care
about what the school and those adults care about.

The second foundational element is that the institution (school, classroom, etc.)
and the adults have to *model the character* that they want to see in the kids. If both
of these things happen, then students are ready to internalize the authentically
endorsed and embodied character that the school hopes they become. Because
modeling is another of our Six Design Principles of PRIMED, the M, we will hold further discussion of this until the next section of the book.

•••••

Four Broad Shifts

Let us start with a school that is entrenched in traditional extrinsic forms of motivation, which tends to rely heavily on giving rewards for character and for leveraging public

displays of affirmation of acts of character. There is a set of four shifts we need to make broadly to move us to effective Intrinsic Motivation. It is a good strategy first to do an audit of all the extrinsic motivators used in the school. Find out who gives out rewards, what they are given for, how often they happen, and what the actual rewards are. Find out who publicly identifies acts or people of character, how and when, etc. Then you can turn to thinking about how to transform as many as possible according to the following four shifts.

(1) The first shift is to move away from material rewards toward social affirmation. Get rid of the things. When Janice Wiley was named Principal of Mann Elementary School, she donated all the rewards stockpiled in the school to the local children's hospital. Instead of giving material rewards for good behavior, start simply letting kids know that you appreciate them and what they did.

(2) Second, move away from pre-ordained consequences to spontaneous ones. Do not announce such consequences in advance, like letting kids know it is your policy to give a sticker to kids who help you clean the room at the end of the day. Instead, catch kids spontaneously in the act of exemplifying good character.

(3) Third, move away from public consequences to private consequences. As we have just discussed, this would be demonstrated by avoiding public affirmation and relying on private affirmation. Putting your hand on a child's shoulder and quietly telling her,

> I am so proud of you. She was so scared. It is her first day in this school. And I saw you go over to her and invite her to sit with you and your friends. That was so kind. Did you see her face? She was beaming with delight. This is what makes this a great school. Keep it up!

Would a child having heard that private message from a valued adult actually need a sticker or a sparkly pencil or an announcement to the entire cafeteria, "Hey everyone! Did you all see what Tanya just did? She is so kind"? The unspoken subtext of course is, "Kinder than any of you. You all should be more like her." I do not think this is what you actually want to communicate.

(4) Fourth, move from irrelevant to relevant consequences. This is particularly true of punishments for undesirable behavior but also applies to positive consequences. There is an old saying, "Make the punishment fit the crime." Or, more broadly, make the consequence fit the behavior. For character development, it should be, "Make the punishment related to the crime." This is at the heart of restorative practices (which we will discuss further below). When a child makes a misstep, the idea is for the consequence to repair the damage, which makes it clearly a matter of relevance. Relevant consequences, in the negative cases, increase the likelihood of learning the reason the misbehavior is undesirable. And in the positive cases, it increases the desired behavior. Just as relevance is important for learning the academic curriculum, it is equally important for "learning" the lessons of character.

Effective Practices for Intrinsic Motivation

The two most important elements in fostering the intrinsic or internal motivation to be and act as a person of character are role modeling and social bonding. This essentially means that we want children who feel emotionally bonded to at least one adult—but ideally more—in the school community as well as to the school community itself. This could be the whole school or some subset of it such as the classroom or grade level. Then we want those adults to whom the students are emotionally bonded and the communities they populate to manifest the character we want to see in the students.

We provided examples of how to promote social bonding in the prior section about Relationships. The second aspect will be covered in the following section on Modeling. Here we will discuss four evidence-based ways to promote Intrinsic Motivation.

Lots of school energy is expended on helping students behave in ways that are safe, prosocial, and conducive to the learning mission of schools. Some of those ways lead to the internalization of values that support being a person who is prosocial and others do not. It is important to understand your true motivation when acting as an educator dealing with a student whose behavior is undesirable. If one truly wants them to internalize prosocial, self-managed values so that they will be intrinsically motivated to be safe, prosocial, etc., then one needs to understand what actually works to lead to such Intrinsic Motivation; that is, where the keys are. Four such strategies follow:

(1) *Restorative*. Traditional behavior management tends to be reactive, retributive/ punitive, and irrelevant. That means it is enacted only after a misbehavior, the goal is to make the transgressor suffer, and the consequences have little or nothing to do with the nature of the misbehavior. There is currently a growing focus on a very different way of thinking about and enacting behavior management. One good example is restorative practices (see the International Institute for Restorative Practices), which includes preventive and reactive elements and aims to repair relationships and the damage done to them while nurturing the development of the transgressor. Marilyn Watson, in her book *Learning to Trust*, has described a related response to misbehavior that she calls Developmental Discipline. The underlying premise is that educators first need to believe that students want to learn and want to flourish. Then educators have to do two fundamental things. First, they need to nurture healthy relationships proactively, both between teacher and student and between students. We have described strategies for this in the prior section on relationships. Second, when a child stumbles, the teacher's stance should be seeing the misbehavior as an opportunity to invest in the child's development to become a more self-managed and prosocial person. This results in more talking about than handing down consequences. When Diane Dymond, Principal of Stix Early Childhood Center School, decided to invest in professional development about developmental discipline with her staff, she noted that the result was a decrease, in discipline situations, of *telling* and an increase in *asking*. Fewer commands and more questions. At Francis Howell Middle School, the students renamed the school discipline policy "TTD," which stood for "Talk to Death." Staff engaged in lengthy dialogues with students about their behavior, often asking questions like, "what else could you have done in that situation?" or "what can you do now to fix the situation?" or "which of our core values did you stumble at?" Some may think of this as "soft" or "going easy" on the students, but it was not infrequent for a Francis Howell Middle student, in the midst of one of these conversations, to plead, "Can you just give me a detention? I don't want to talk about this anymore." In fact, Restorative Practices offers a very useful set of questions to use in such situations (https://store.iirp.edu/restorative-questions-cards-pack-of-100-english-or-spanish/).

(2) *Empathy Promotion*. Induction is a widely studied and impactful implementation strategy in child development (both in child-rearing and in education). It essentially is a way of constructing evaluative messages whether one is trying to laud or to criticize a child's behavior. Induction messages need to have the following elements. First, there is the evaluative message, some version of either "I am so proud of/pleased with you …" or "I am so angry/frustrated/disappointed with you …" Second, there must be a clear justification for the evaluation, as in "…

because X." Third, the justification must include mention of the consequences of the child's behavior, such as "because it is now broken and useless" or "because it now works better than it ever did before." Lastly, the impact on another's feelings should be highlighted: "Because it is now broken and useless, and he is so sad about it he is crying" or "because it now works better than it ever did before and he is so thrilled to be able to use it so well now." Induction has been found to lead to an impressive set of character outcomes related to Intrinsic Motivation such as the tendency to be more altruistic and to have a stronger conscience.

(3) *Focus on Effort.* When using rewards or, preferably, praise, the focus should be the child's effort rather than the quality or quantity of the outcomes of that effort. One of the rules to follow is that rewarding or praising outcome increases the likelihood of repeating that outcome (e.g., a good grade on a math test, accruing more service hours, etc.) but also increases any path to that outcome (e.g., hard work, studying, lying, cheating, etc.). On the other hand, praising effort increases the Intrinsic Motivation to work hard, including internalizing GRIT, which is persistence at a task with passion.

(4) *Character as a Self-project.* Humans, at least in part, are self-constructed. We have will, we can project over time including into the future through foresight, and we can be self-evaluative. Reflection, in the case of character especially about oneself, is a critical tool for constructing one's own character. Furthermore, especially in adolescence and beyond, the formation of one's sense of self, one's identity, is critically important to one's character formation. Educators should provide the time, inclination, and competencies necessary for students to reflect on their own character, their sociomoral behaviors, and their identities. We will return to this issue in the later section on Developmental Pedagogy.

● ● ● ● ●

Resources for Intrinsic Motivation

Books

Duckworth, A. (2016). *GRIT: The Power of Passion and Perseverance.* New York: Scribner.
Kohn, A. (1999). *Punished by Rewards: The Trouble with Gold Stars, Incentive Plans, A's, Praise, and Other Bribes.* Boston: Houghton Mifflin.
Watson, M. (2019). *Learning to Trust: Attachment Theory and Classroom Management* (2nd Edition). New York: Oxford University Press.

Websites

International Institute for Restorative Practices—https://store.iirp.edu
Self-Determination Theory—www.selfdeterminationtheory.org

PRIMED Action Planning Worksheet:

Intrinsic Motivation Strategies

Intrinsic Motivation: Valuing something for its own sake and not for its consequences (e.g., rewards, punishment, recognition). Internalizing values so they apply wherever one is (not just in school or in the presence of monitoring adults). Leads to doing the right thing even when one no one is watching.

Evidence-based implementation strategies:

Behavior management:	Developmental discipline
	Induction/Empathy
	Praise effort, not ability
	Use of reflection (especially moral)
Self-growth:	Challenging/Meaningful/Relevant Curriculum
	Opportunities for revising one's work/efforts
	Goal setting/Imagining possible selves
Service:	Opportunities for moral action
	Community service/Service learning

STEP ONE:

Please identify at least two Intrinsic Motivation strategies that are already in place in your school/district. You may use the previous categories or anything else you do that you think increases the internalization of character and values.

1.

2.

3.

4.

STEP TWO:

Please identify at least two more things you can do that would increase the Intrinsic Motivation of students in your school/district. Again, you can choose from the previous list or list anything else you think would be good for you to implement for the purpose of increased internalization of character and values.

1.

2.

3.

4.

PRIMED Principle 4: Modeling

17

●●●●●

Being Good

As Tom Lickona has pointed out, "the single most powerful tool you have to influence a child's character . . . is your character." Hence, character education starts in your mirror. For character education to work optimally, it must start with the adults who impact the students. Moreover, they must start in a very uncomfortable place, by looking in the mirror—in the stark light of honesty—and assess their own character. Then they must grapple with the blemishes, the impurities of character, that we all will inevitably see in ourselves.

Children tend to learn more from what we do than what we say they should do. As Ralph Waldo Emerson has been paraphrased to say, "Your actions speak so loudly that I cannot hear a word you are saying."

Students, particularly after the early primary grades, are not only good at seeing hypocrisy in the adults around them . . . they yearn for it. They want to see adults' faults, limitations, and stumbles. Particularly the adolescents, who psychologically need to convince themselves they are at least peers with the adults, whether it be parents/caretakers or educators or anyone else. For them to psychologically establish themselves as "mature," in whatever that means to them, they need to see adults as no better than they see themselves. Then they can feel they have attained maturity. Noting the limitations, stumbles, and weaknesses of adults is fuel for their psychological growth. They are hypocrisy detectives and they do not need our help giving them ammo for their attack on alleged adult superiority.

It behooves us, as adults around children impacting their character, to try to be our best selves and to model what we want our students to become. In the case of educators, with a purpose of helping them flourish, we need to do this deliberatively. Think of it this way. If a school commits to a set of core character strengths, such as respect, responsibility, honesty, compassion, and justice—and if it systematically urges students to embody those strengths—then we do damage to our noble enterprise of character education if we ourselves demonstrate disrespect, act irresponsibly, tell lies, are insensitive to the plight of others, or show favoritism or prejudice. We undermine the entire enterprise of character education through our behaviors that are antithetical to what we demand in children. We simply cannot demand more from children than we demand from ourselves and expect to influence their character development for the good.

None of us are perfect. None of us can be 100% respectful or compassionate. We all will slip for one reason or another. The request here is not to be a saint but to be the best person you can, with the full clear realization that you will never attain perfection. And to keep striving to be even a little bit better than you already are, but to forgive yourself for not being perfect. In other words, and we will delve deeper into this in the section on Developmental Pedagogy, make your character a self-project, but learn to continue to love yourself as the imperfect person you are. Always aim for perfection, but never expect it. Moreover, always own your missteps (what better manifestation of responsibility?) and be open and forthcoming about that. Negative modeling is toxic, but the antidote is heartfelt apology.

There are three ways in which it is important to understand that everyone in the school—and the institution itself—falls under the mandate, paraphrasing Gandhi's dictum to be the change we want to see in the world, to be the character we want to see in students. First, they are always watching and do not miss much. The title of Ted and Nancy Sizer's wonderful book on high schools is *The Students are Watching*. Indeed they are. And not just in high school. I often think that teachers subconsciously believe that they each have a self-activating Harry Potter Cloak of Invisibility that clicks on when they do not want students to hear what they say and/or see what they do and then clicks off when they want to be heard and seen. I am sorry to break it to you, but you do not have one. No one does.

Students see and hear all you do and say and remember it. It has a powerful impact on them. You undermine your values and messages when you tell students to be responsible and you lose their papers or fail to return them when you promise you will. Or when you chastise them for lying or cheating and likely penalize them as well, and then you lie to them about why you did not grade their papers or were absent on Tuesday. Or when you teach justice and compassion and show favoritism toward certain students or, perhaps even worse, certain subgroups of students. And students do not only see you at school; they see you in the community at the mall or restaurant or grocery store, and they are still watching.

As Aristotle pointed out over two millennia ago, all adults who are around children will impact their character, whether we like it, intend it, or not. And a significant way we impact them is by what we model. Second, being a role model is not a personal choice. Many years ago, Charles Barkley, the Hall of Fame basketball player and now sports announcer, declared that he is not a role model and in effect was imploring kids not to choose him as a role model. He knew his own character weaknesses and did not want youth to emulate him as a person just because he was a great athlete and entertainer. He was wise enough to realize that being a role model is not a personal choice. Rather it is up to the person who emulates you. You have no say in that.

Third, we never know which of our actions or statements will have an impact on a child's journey nor on which children. All adults working in schools ultimately serve as role models, and we do not know which students are impacted most by our character and behavior. We all need to be cognizant of this and be vigilant about what we are modeling. Educators frequently tell me of students who come back to them—often many years later—and tell them of the profound impact they had on that former student's life, even saving that life. Moreover, frequently the teacher had no idea and sometimes does not even remember the student. It is important to note that some of those impacts were positive: Affirming, uplifting, inspiring. However, others were harmful: Stigmatizing, ostracizing, and diminishing of self-worth. You just never know. It can be something you said or did in a matter of seconds and do not even remember later that day.

Being a model of character is rather a lot to ask of educators and others who work with or around kids. Being asked to be a paragon of virtue, a moral exemplar, a pedagogical saint, is asking quite a lot. And you can rightfully argue that you are not paid enough to be one (and you are correct), that you do not have enough recognition and social status by virtue of being an educator to be held to such a lofty ethical and social standard (and you are correct in most parts of the world).

However, being an educator is not merely a job. It is not even merely a profession. Certainly, it is a job and a profession, but it is also ultimately a calling. And it is no less a calling than the calling to religious life or to the profession of arms. When one is called, then social status and remuneration are not the most important issues, although both are important. Educators are called. They are called to service. They are called to service toward nurturing the flourishing (and learning) of the students in their charge. So being asked to model character is far from unreasonable. In fact, it is central to fulfilling the calling to education, which brings us full circle back to the P in PRIMED . . . your Priority or Purpose.

18

•••••

The Pedagogy of Modeling

There are two broad categories of implementation strategies for leveraging role modeling to nurture the flourishing of human goodness in students. One is to increase the likelihood that the people they encounter in the school community are positive role models. The other is to expose them to depictions of role models, e.g., in literature and history.

•••••

Role Models in the School Environment

All adults who work with or around kids are models, whether positive or negative, of character. Hence, we need strategies to maximize the degree to which those adults actually model good character. In any organization, there are two basic paths to adult character—or professional competency—for that matter: Selection and formation. Whether one wants teachers of character or is looking for new members of a religious order, police recruits, customer service representatives, or recruits for a sports team, one needs to look at how you screen and select them (selection) and how you invest in their personal and professional development once you bring them on board (formation). Neither is simple nor easy.

There are no simple litmus tests of character. While there are many good questionnaires that reliably assess various aspects of character, they are suited for group assessment and not individual diagnosis. Nonetheless, wise school leaders still try to identify applicants who fit the school ethos and character mission. They want such people as members of the school community because they will be better at their jobs, for example, at teaching children. However, they should also be looking for people who would be good role models for the students in their journeys to character flourishing. In his excellent brief history of *Moral Education in America*, B. Edward McClellan points out that, as teaching migrated from the household to the schoolhouse, women were chosen as teachers mainly because it was felt that they would be better moral role models for students.

Mostly this selection is implemented in the interview process. For instance, you might propose challenging classroom or behavior management situations to applicants and ask them questions like, "Have you ever faced a situation like this? And if so, how did you handle it?" or "What would you do in such a situation? Why that?" Kristen Pelster has said, "I don't ask them about their content expertise. If they have a certification in math education or science education, then I assume they know the content or could learn more. I ask them about character education." As a saying from the business sector goes, "People get hired for their knowledge and skills. They get fired for their character." Why not try to minimize the latter by screening for it?

Another strategy is simply to observe them with students. Some schools ask applicants to prepare and deliver a lesson to a class or have student interview teams and ask the applicants to spend a half hour or so simply talking with the students and then getting the students' feedback on their impressions of the applicant.

One clever principal told me he asks applicants to describe their first day of school in the classroom. I think this can provide a novel and important window into the applicant's priorities and philosophy of education and the degree to which they are truly child-centered and relational. After all, Prioritization and Relationships are two of the Design Principles of PRIMED.

Schools usually have a small "search committee" composed of leadership and select teachers. One strategy would be to expand that committee to get more perspectives, for example, parents and support staff and even students. Another strategy from the world of business is to populate the committee with those people who most deeply understand and embrace the school purpose (mission, vision), for they will be most likely to focus on and weight the characteristics of a teacher with the potential to be a great role model and character educator.

Another selection strategy is self-selection. Some principals write their philosophy of education, essentially a Priorities manifesto or statement of Noble Purpose, describing the kind of school they are trying to nurture and shepherd. In one case, it was heavily focused on whole-child education and nurturing the flourishing of human goodness. In other, it was self-disclosure about a tough life journey that led to committing to serving children and goodness. The rationale was to let applicants know the kind of place to which they were applying to work and the leader's expectations of all adults in the school. He sent this to all applicants before he called any in for interviews. Ideally, those who disagreed might choose not to apply. It is a great idea as a school leader to articulate your philosophy, vision, and purpose even if it is not used in staff selection. However, why not use it for that? It could even be used as part of the interview process.

Remember the previous saying: "People get hired for their knowledge and skills. They get fired for their character"? Or rather their lack of good character. Many things mitigate against screening out bad character. One is that there are no foolproof screening devices. Another is that we are all imperfect beings, and so everyone you hire will be flawed in multiple ways. The goal here is to minimize the degree that those flaws are fatal and residing in fundamental character (especially moral character).

One solution to this quandary is the second overall strategy for maximizing positive role models in the school, namely, formation. By this we mean one of two things: (1) the personal and professional development around character of the adults to whom the children are exposed in the school setting or (2) creating the motivation and structures for those adults to make their own character formation/improvement a self-project.

In either case, ideally the school has or develops an ethos of adult character growth. Moreover, this ethos needs to be a widely expected and supported way of being among all adults, not just the new hires.

Becoming aware of the need for self-examination and character growth of course is necessary before one can commit to it. Socrates claimed that the unexamined life is not worth living. The staff at Francis Howell Middle School came to this through the strong focus of their principal. At Fox High School (St. Louis), this happened from a grassroots level. Three teachers went to a workshop where "The List" was presented. This was a list of ways that even good teachers bully students. This startled them in two ways. First, bullying in schools is usually thought of as a student-to-student phenomenon, not as something adults do. Second, even these excellent teachers saw themselves reflected in some of the examples; they realized that they had been bul-lying students without even knowing it. They came back to school and presented it to the staff, who were equally stunned. This led to a courageous and powerful video in which they describe some of these ways of bullying and describe their own trans-gressions and insights. You can find it on YouTube (*Fox High School The List*). I use it frequently for professional development and staff discussions on the topic of adult modeling.

Tom Lickona and Matt Davidson, in their report *Smart and Good High Schools*, describe what they call a Professional Ethical Learning Community (PELC). The staff of a school needs to be a certain sort of community (professional, ethical, learning) with all the practices and norms that support that. This builds on the great work con-cerning Professional Learning Communities from Rick DuFour and his colleagues. PLCs focus on academic instruction, however, and Lickona and Davidson expand that to include moral character. They list six principles of the PELC:

(1) Developed shared purpose and identity.
(2) Align practices with desired outcomes and relevant research.
(3) Have a voice; take a stand.
(4) Take personal responsibility for continuous self-development.
(5) Practice collective responsibility for excellence and ethics.
(6) Grapple with the tough issues—the elephants in the living room.

These principles align closely with many of the messages in this book. It all starts with purpose (Prioritization). It then needs to apply evidence-based practices aligned with those priorities. People need to be empowered (the fifth Design Principle of PRIMED). Besides administrator-led character development, everyone needs to make it a self-project (the sixth Design Principle . . . Developmental Pedagogy), but we also need to support each other and be a community of character. And we need to have the courage to grap-ple with tough issues, like admitting when our "character crowns" are slipping.

If the staff are to become courageous and dedicated to personal improvement, then the school leadership must model that. In other words, for staff to model character, they need to intentionally be character, including personal growth. If they are to do that, then the leader needs to model openness, humility, and personal growth. Kevin Navarro, the Principal of Greensboro Montessori School (North Carolina) has identi-fied what he calls the Vulnerable Leader, part of the model of the Connected Leader we explored in the chapter on leadership. The Vulnerable Leader has three main charac-teristics: Humility; openness; authenticity. A vulnerable leader would be a model for self-growth for the entire staff.

Another form of formation is professional development. Julie Frugo, Head of School at Premier Charter School (St. Louis), a National School of Character, focused her dis-sertation on the characteristics of a Professional Growth Leader. Such leaders invest in three components: (1) building learning capacity; (2) empowering teachers; (3) nur-turing a positive adult culture. In her own school, she has created an innovative and extensive three-year program for the professional development of teachers new to the school, which was described in the leadership chapter.

Goal setting is an important part of self-development. We will address this from the perspective of student self-development in the final Design Principle of PRIMED, Developmental Pedagogy, later in this book. However, for adults in the school com-munity this is often included in the teacher/staff evaluation processes. However, the focus is usually on academic pedagogy, unless there is a behavior problem, such as ineffective behavior management, tardiness, or poor record keeping. A good idea is to ask each staff member to set personal character goals for the year. As with any goal setting, those goals should be relevant and realistic, and the school needs to provide scaffolding and monitoring to support the educator's growth journey. Such scaffolding can include a structure like a strategic planning form, regular check-ins or reporting, and social supports like small staff groups or accountability buddies.

Merle Schwartz, in one of the very few studies of the modeling of character educators, identified seven characteristics of teachers who are role models of character for their students:

(1) Show moral concern for others.
(2) Act out of a commitment to the development of others.
(3) Show integrity through consistency between words and actions.
(4) Is forgiving (self and other).
(5) Demonstrates self-reflection and reasoning competency.
(6) Self-control in service of others.
(7) Empathy and perspective-taking.

She also found that high school teachers who were rated highest by their students on these characteristics also showed the characteristics of transformational leadership and emotional competence. Indeed, this offers a recipe for both selection and formation of role models in our schools.

Now that we have focused on the role modeling of the people populating the school community, let us turn to a discussion of studying role models. Before we do, however, it is important to note that it is not only adults who are role models in the school. Other students are as well. Older students are role models for younger students all the time. Many schools make this explicit to the students; that is, that they have to manifest good character because the younger kids are watching them, and they are role models. It is not unusual to hear students in such schools spontaneously talking about the impact they have as role models for younger students. Finally, age is not always unidirectional here. At Barretts Elementary School in St. Louis, a fourth-grade class asked their first grade "buddies" to teach them how to be leaders. You see, that first-grade teacher had made leadership a curricular priority in her classroom, and by buddying with that first grade class the fourth graders had become aware of this and reached out to their little buddies as teachers, experts in leadership, and role models.

● ● ● ● ●

Studying Role Models

Schools already focus on studying role models in so many ways. They populate our social studies curricula. Most pieces of literature have characters who are potential role models. In the arts, we study the character of the creators of the art and music. And the characters depicted in art or music. In physical education, we learn about "super stars" and often also look at their character and grapple with how to model good sportsmanship, both from those that do and those that fail to do so.

Here we will simply address a few other ways to do this that can supplement what is already being done. One is to adopt a curriculum that is designed to focus on role models. Perhaps the best one is the Giraffe Project. It is the brainchild of Ann Medlock and John Graham. It has materials ranging from early childhood education through high school and is focused on three fundamental stages. First, the students study role models. In this situation, they are studying an extensive but unique set of role models . . . giraffes. The giraffe metaphor is intended to underscore people who put themselves at risk to serve others . . . people who, like a giraffe, "stick their necks out." Ann and John have, for a long time, been soliciting and vetting nominations of giraffes from around the world and now have over 1,300 on their website (www.giraffe.org). These include famous people and relatively unknown people, children and adults. Once they study them, they can turn to discovering giraffes in their own communities, people who have done heroic altruistic acts (such as going to jail for social justice, saving lives in a fire or flood) and live among them. Finally, they are encouraged to become a giraffe by engaging in service to others. The best news is that now that Ann and John are facing retirement, the entire curriculum is online free.

A second example of a role model curriculum is Character Development and Leadership, created by Joe Hoedel who started this originally in his own high school classrooms. It now also has a middle school version (www.characterandleadership.com). It focuses on 18 character strengths, with a curriculum for each. Each strength is embodied by a role model who exemplifies that characteristic. Research has shown the effectiveness of this curriculum in reducing antisocial behaviors and increasing prosocial behaviors and attitudes.

Identifying role models is a great project for a librarian/media specialist. Schools can enlist their expertise in identifying and cataloging books and other media that depict role models. If the school has an explicit set of character values/goals/virtues/strengths, they can be identified by which of those the specific instance of media covers. Classroom teachers or curriculum specialists can then enlist the collaboration of the media specialists in identifying books and other media for a specific audience or curricular area.

In the section on Developmental Pedagogy, we will describe Inspire/Aspire in more detail as a self-growth structure for students. Part of this is to identify a role model for a self-chosen growth goal such as integrity or respect and to write an essay about that person. Doing so is a way to inspire and concretize one's own personal goals for character development. The adults can do the same. At the US Air Force Academy, each class (grade level) selects a role model for the entire group of approximately 1,000 cadets for their four years there.

● ● ● ● ●

Concluding Remarks

Character education is fundamentally about being, with and around others. Hence the models that students are exposed to, both in their daily interactions with other members of the school community and through study of the lives of others, is critical to their character journeys. This is why modeling is one of the Six Design Principles of PRIMED. Schools that want to be effective at nurturing the flourishing of human goodness in their students will have to tackle the often-challenging issue of the "way of being" of those in the school community, especially themselves. Going back to Ralph Waldo Emerson's challenge and our paraphrase of Gandhi, we need to be the character we want to see developing in our students. Since you do not have a self-activating Harry Potter Cloak of Invisibility, that means all the time. Being strategic, intentional, and effective at this as a school is your only viable option.

•••••

Resources for Modeling

Readings

DuFour, R., & Eaker, R. (1998). *Professional Learning Communities at Work: Best Practices for Enhancing Student Achievement*. Bloomington, IN: Solution Tree.

Hoedel, J.M. (2005). *Role Models: Examples of Character and Leadership*. Greensboro, NC: Character Development Group.

Lickona, T., & Davidson, M. (2007). *Smart and Good High Schools: Integrating Excellence and Ethics for Success in School, Work and Beyond*. Washington, DC: Character Education Partnership. (for PDF: http://www2.cortland.edu/centers/character/high-schools/)

McClellan, B.E. (1999). *Moral Education in America: Schools and the Shaping of Character from Colonial Times to the Present*. New York: Teachers College Press.

Palmer, P. (2017). *The Courage to Teach: Exploring the Inner Landscape of a Teacher's Life*. New York: Wiley.

Schwartz, M.J. (2007). The modeling of moral character for teachers: Behaviors, characteristics, and dispositions that may be taught. *Journal of Research in Character Education*, 5(1), 1–28.

Sizer, T., & Sizer, N.F. (2000). *The Students are Watching: Schools and the Moral Contract*. Boston: Beacon Press.

Videos and Websites

Character Leadership—www.characterleadership.com

"The List"—Fox High School—www.youtube.com/watch?v=b6MSE5voYkU

The Giraffe Project—www.giraffe.org

PRIMED Action Planning Worksheet:

Modeling Strategies

Modeling: Acting in ways that are consistent with and embody the character goals of the school/district. This is especially important for the adults in the school but applies to all who serve as role models to students (e.g., older students).

Evidence-based implementation strategies:

    Role modeling/mentoring

    Studying others as role models/exemplars

STEP ONE:

Please identify at least two Modeling strategies that are already in place in your school/ district. You may use the two strategy categories presented earlier or anything else you do that you think increases the degree to which potential role models embody character in general and specifically the school or district's explicit vision of character.

    1.

    2.

    3.

    4.

STEP TWO:

Please identify at least two more things you can do that would increase the modeling of character in your school/district. Again, you can choose from the two previous categories or list anything else you think would be good for you to implement for the purpose of increased role modeling of character.

    1.

    2.

    3.

    4.

Part VI

PRIMED Principle 5:
Empowerment

19

• • • • •

What Is Empowerment and Why Is It Important for Character Education?

What do we mean by Empowerment? A good metaphor is "voice," both literal and figurative voice. Literal voice is speaking. But it entails hearing others. Listening to them and caring about the voices of others, their perspectives, insights, opinions, knowledge, needs and desires, reasoning, etc. To do that optimally, one needs to do more than listen when they share. It means paying attention to them and hearing them in a deep way. It means respecting their perspectives, even if you disagree. We can see clearly how the political division of the US—and many other countries—has led to a dearth of listening across divides.

That is a lot to ask, but there is more to literal voice. It also entails creating the conditions for voices to emerge and be heard, which should start with authentically wanting to hear others' voices and then making that not only possible but also likely. That includes creating conditions and spaces for voice. In the last chapter on Empowerment, we will see many ways schools can do this. Examples include regular class meetings, authentic student government, and reforming staff meetings to be more discursive. Literal voice also means being authentically invitational of the voices of others, particularly of those who are reticent to speak or share their inner lives. This may be because they do not believe that anyone really cares about it or that it feels perilous to open up and chime in. Alternatively, it could be for reasons of individual personality or small group dynamics or for a host of other reasons that make speaking about things that matter less likely. We need to create moments, cultures, and relationships that authentically invite the voices of others.

Figurative voice is more about power, not that literal voice itself is not potentially powerful. But power comes in lots of places and ways. We often ask educators to complete school staff surveys that include questions about power. Questions like, "Who makes the decisions in this place?", "Do you have any say in important decisions?", and "How do you feel about how decisions are made here?" Of course, the answers vary widely. Some schools appear to be top down in power and decision making, and, generally, staff do not like that. There are, of course, exceptions. At Brentwood Middle School (eventually a National School of Character), when Julie Sperry was the principal, the small cohesive staff staunchly resisted shared decision making. Sperry was trying to empower them and be more democratic, and they were having none of it. They preferred that she tell them what to do. The breakthrough there came through the principal strategically building closer relationships with each staff member and learning to be a servant leader, that is, serving the growth of each of the staff members.

Only then were they willing to share ownership and leadership of the school, which was the path to reaching excellence in character education.

Some schools already have wider power distribution. Decisions are made at least in part based upon surveys of the relevant stakeholders, by staff open discussions, and by giving other staff the authority to take control of specific decisions or other aspects of the school. Rarer are fully democratic schools, where decisions are made collectively. When I worked in the Just Community Schools project at the Harvard Graduate School of Education in the 1970s with a great team of scholars led by Professor Lawrence Kohlberg, we were trying to implement radically democratic communities in high schools in the Boston area and later in New York. This was never easy, but it was powerful. I recommend the book *Lawrence Kohlberg's Approach to Moral Education* by Clark Power, Ann Higgins, and Lawrence Kohlberg as a detailed description of this innovative journey to empowerment and character.

There are many challenges in sharing power. A long time ago, the economics department at Yale University tried to be fully democratic and found that it was simply inefficient. Too many trivial decisions, like purchasing office supplies, were eating up too much group time and would be better dispatched by an administrator. Empowerment needs to be executed appropriately.

This becomes clearer when one considers the fact that, while my examples thus far are about the educators in the school, I am actually advocating empowerment of *all* stakeholders in the school community, including children and support staff. For children there are a few points that are important to consider. First, they need to be empowered too. Second, there are clear biases against empowering children. These biases are based on false beliefs that they are incapable, too immature, too irresponsible, and that chaos will ensue if students are given control.

There is a concept called adultism, which is essentially a prejudice against children. The core of the adultist prejudice is treating children as incompetent and dependent—often out of a true feeling of love—but resulting in viewing and interacting with children in a condescending, disempowering, and even dismissive way. Children can usually do much more than we believe. I always marvel at the fact that when I advocate giving students more power, voice, say in how the classroom or school functions, high schools tell me that, "Well our strongest 11th and 12th graders could probably do that, but our 9th graders are too immature." And the middle schools tell me that, "Well our best 8th graders could probably do it, but our 6th graders are too immature." And the elementary schools tell me that, "our 5th graders could do it, and perhaps our strongest 4th graders, but our students in the earlier grades couldn't." I hope you see the issue here. Why can fifth graders be trusted with voice and power in the elementary school but the next year in middle school as sixth graders they cannot? Ditto for the eighth and ninth graders. In fact, they can all do it. Denise Funston and Tina Basler, Principals of primary grade schools (Windsor Elementary and Plattin Primary, respectively) for five- through eight-year-olds empower all their kids while giving more responsibility to the second graders (ages seven through eight). People tend to rise to your expectations and sink to your expectations. Set them high and provide supports.

Third, there are good reasons for empowering children, for their developmental benefits. We will examine those in the next chapter.

Fourth, as respect and responsibility are two of the most common values on the focal list of schools, listening to others is a primary way of showing respect for them. Moreover, giving them authentic voice is building responsibility. As Tom Lickona says, respect is a two-way street. You foster respect in part by giving respect.

Some of the defining elements of empowerment are:

- Believing in the competency and worth of others and soliciting and listening to their thoughts.
- Enabling and encouraging others to participate authentically in or control decision making.
- Being open to the input of others.
- Being willing to change and innovate.
- Recognizing others for their contributions.
- Sharing leadership with others.

If that did not convince you of the importance of empowerment for character education, let us look at four compelling reasons for why empowerment matters and deserves to be one of the Six Design Principles of PRIMED.

(1) *Empowerment is a fundamental psychological need.* Self-determination Theory contends that autonomy (having a voice) is a fundamental human need. The leaders of SDT, Deci and Ryan, have specifically focused on schooling, identifying the significant positive power of "autonomy-supportive" schools and classrooms on student learning and psychological development. One particularly interesting finding came from a study by a group of researchers from Australia, England, Iran, and Finland (led by Nikos Chatzisarantis and published in *Contemporary Educational Psychology* in 2019). These scholars reported that affording autonomy equally among students leads to optimal outcomes both for human flourishing and for academic achievement. In other words, meeting the basic need for empowerment for all students is an optimal way to serve the two main goals of education: Learning and development. In an even deeper sense, it feeds the fundamental human need to be known and cared about. As David Augsburger said in his book, *Caring Enough to Hear and Be Heard*, "Being heard is so close to being loved that for the average person they are almost indistinguishable."

(2) *Empowering others is a duty.* The philosopher Immanuel Kant and more recently John Rawls among others argued that the central ethical principle is respect for personhood. The most central guideline for deciding how to act morally is whether one is acting in accordance with a sense of respect for all persons involved. As I like to remind educators, "Kids are people too." They may be smaller and less fully developed, but every single one of them is no less a person. Hence, they deserve, in fact are ethically owed, respect just as any other person is. And empowerment is a way to respect others. This is where adultism goes awry.

(3) *Empowerment is necessary for flourishing democracies.* For democracy to be maximally effective as what John Dewey called "a mode of associated living," it would need people who both want to and have the capacity to live well together. As both John Dewey and Walter Parker have argued, such people do not grow on trees or materialize out of thin air, nor can you order them online. Both democratic citizens and ethical people—and we want both—need to be cultivated. That is where character education comes in. Parker also offers an important insight through the word "idiot." It originated in classic Greek times as a pejorative term for people who acted out of self-interest and not as a citizen concerned with the common good. As we look at democracies around the world struggling today, we can see the increase in the electorate voting as "idiots" in this sense. Empowering character education is a potential counterweight to that selfish tendency. To revisit my

belief in long-term human moral progress and to borrow from Reverend Martin Luther King, *the arc of human history bends slowly toward justice only because humans are becoming more moral.*

(4)   *Empowered education is good education.* Pedro Noguera has argued that many schools, at least in the United States, are better at preparing students for a life in prison than for a life in a healthy world. Schools often share more with prisons than they do with democratic society. They tend to be disempowering, demeaning, punitive, and controlling places where voices are silenced. Schools need to understand that for students to learn and develop, such an environment is remarkably suboptimal. When we introduced the aphorism that "good character education is good education," we noted that there is an abundance of data showing that character education and social-emotional learning lead to better academic achievement. People frequently wonder why. Well a big part of it is that such schools tend to respect students and make spaces for their voices to matter in a wide variety of ways. And they empower teachers, parents, and other stakeholders. In such schools, students want to be there, feel a valued member of a community, and therefore work harder and behave better.

20

●●●●●

Empowerment Implementation Strategies

In our review of *What Works in Character Education*, we have identified four main evidence-based implementation strategies for Empowerment:

(1) Shared leadership.
(2) Democratic classrooms.
(3) Culture of empowerment/collaboration.
(4) Fair and respectful treatment of students.

We will examine and detail the specific implementation methods for each one. Before we begin, it is important to recall the intersection of the Design Principles of PRIMED. For empowerment to happen optimally and most productively, it needs to (1) include all stakeholders in the school community, (2) be built upon a network of healthy relationships, (3) be an authentic priority of the school philosophy and approach, and (4) be modeled by school leadership, especially the principal. Certainly, a classroom teacher can be empowering in a school that is not. And other subunits of the school, such as grade levels, departments, or middle school teams, can do likewise. Ideally, as Character.org's third principle of *The 11 Principles Framework for Schools* demands for character education in general, it should be "comprehensive, intentional, and proactive" and "infused throughout the school day."

●●●●●

Shared Leadership

Sharing leadership roles, duties, and authority is central to a pedagogy of empowerment or empowerment in any domain. It runs through the Character.org *11 Principles Framework for Schools* and is an explicit idea in nearly half of the Principles. Principle 5 encourages empowering students to be moral agents in the school and beyond by engaging in "moral action," an idea that is echoed in Principle 7 (which is also about the I in PRIMED). Principle 8 suggests sharing responsibility for character with the staff in a "learning and moral community." Principle 9 is focally about "shared moral leadership" among the administration, an inclusive character education leadership committee, particularly among students. Principle 10 encourages schools to engage "families and community members as partners."

As discussed in the section on Modeling, this journey starts with the school leader, and it begins in the mirror. Leaders need to examine themselves and their leadership styles to understand the degree to which they are modeling empowerment. When the participants in our Leadership Academy in Character Education survey their staff about the adult culture in the school, they often report that staff complain that all-important decisions are made by the school and/or district leadership. Another complaint is that their opinions are solicited but that they do not believe they are heeded; for example, that the decision was made before staff were asked to chime in. Some of this is actually revealing feigned empowerment, but some of it is due to faulty communication. That is, the findings in staff (and other) surveys may actually lead to change, but those surveyed are not made aware of the connection between their input and authentic change. Transparency is critical.

Leaders can self-examine in a number of ways. First, they can simply do a reflective internal inventory of the degree to which they want to and actually do empower others and who is omitted. In fact, the servant leadership model we presented in the chapter on leadership includes Empowerment explicitly as one of the eight virtues of Melinda Bier's CViL (Cultivating Virtues in Leaders) model of servant leadership. In our CEEL project, we guide leaders through self-evaluation and then strategic planning for personal/professional growth on each of the virtues, including empowerment.

Second, leaders can ask others the degree to which they authentically empower other stakeholders, as we require in our Leadership Academy. This takes courage, a servant leadership virtue. If you are even more courageous, I suggest then sharing the tabulated results, still anonymous of course, with the staff and using these data for a Professional Learning Community (PLC) type school improvement discussion.

Third, you can engage a leadership coach to help with understanding and nurturing your own empowerment of others. If you find a good coach who understands empowering leadership, then you will likely gain insights you might have missed in self-analysis. Often a good mentor can be very helpful in this regard as well, as long as the mentor understands and values an empowering leadership style.

Fourth, you can utilize scientific leadership style assessment instruments to identify some of your tendencies. We have been using measures of servant leadership in our leadership development programs lately. You can also use other leadership inventories of related concepts like Transformational Leadership or Connected Leadership.

Once you have a handle on the degree to which you actually engage in empowering leadership, you can begin to cultivate it more deeply by being more systematic in the way you already do it and by expanding the scope of your empowerment of others, where you empower, how much you empower, and who is empowered.

Where You Empower

Are there some domains where you empower others, for example, delivering in-house professional development or discipline/behavior management? And others where you do not, for example, budgeting, hiring, or crafting school reports to the school district authorities? In some cases, this may be fully appropriate, even mandated, and in other cases, it just became a routine about which you never reflected. In yet other cases, it may be simply "offloading" onerous tasks like discipline or dealing with uncooperative parents. It is important to know why you empower in some places and not others. Being perceived as not trusting staff to do some things they could easily do or not listening to their perspectives and advice in those areas can seriously erode staff trust, and that is highly corrosive of school excellence, both academically and developmentally. This is precisely the issue we discussed earlier of staff culture. Furthermore, for those leaders who want to be what Julie Frugo, Head of School of Premier Charter School in St. Louis, calls a "professional growth leader" and to cultivate future school leaders among staff, sharing the more challenging aspects of leadership is excellent mentoring and apprenticeship for emerging leaders.

How Much You Empower

It is important to consider the notion of delegation when one considers empowerment and to distinguish between authentic and inauthentic delegation. Authentic delegation is giving another responsibility because you believe they can handle it and, typically, because you think they and others will benefit from their added responsibility. As the leader, you will have their backs when they need your support. If funding or staff time becomes necessary, you will try to make that happen. When staff push back, you will step forward and show solidarity and that the delegation has your support. Inauthentic delegation is often offloading tasks you do not want to do, think are relatively unimportant, or even controversial and fraught with peril. Then when the person to whom you have delegated needs your support, you do not come through. Perhaps your true priorities trump these needs or you do not want to be associated with the controversial issues. In one large suburban school district, when character education first got traction, it was assigned to school counselors and, sometimes, assistant principals, because no one thought it was important enough to land on the desk of the lead principal. In most cases, this failed, at least so far as being comprehensive and school-wide, and the delegated staff were burning out from trying to get others on board. Authentic delegation is empowering and supports character education. Inauthentic delegation is harmful to the adult culture of the school, models poor leadership, and essentially undermines effective character education and education generally. When schools do include different groups in character education, they include some stakeholder groups, particularly those who are not professional educators, just by assigning them character-related duties and tasks. Rather than giving the office staff or the kitchen staff character education responsibilities, consider empowering them more deeply by asking them to think of ways they can support character education and the school's character education initiative in their own respective domains.

Whom You Empower

Ideally, having an expansive notion of who the school stakeholders are and including all groups and as many members of the groups as possible is a powerful school improvement and character education strategy. The most obvious groups are the school leadership team and the certified (professional) educators in the school. However, it also includes the students and their parents/guardians. Often, the common groups that get ignored in empowerment—and other strategies—are (1) support staff (such as clerical staff, custodial staff, bus drivers, food service workers, etc.), (2) parents, and (3) local community members who have a vested interest in how well you implement character education (such as local law enforcement, residential neighbors, local business owners, local government, etc.). All too often, some or all of these groups are left out, underrepresented, or assigned tasks in a hierarchical fashion. This often happens because we do not think of them or because we do not feel comfortable sharing power with them. Look at your lead character education team for example and ask yourself which of these groups are not represented. I do recommend adding at least two of each group, so they can support each other. Another issue is who represents such groups. Often we pick outliers. We select our "superstar" students or the parents who are the officers of the parent organization. Or we pick members who really have two or more connections to the school—for example a secretary who has two children in the school or a local official who is married to a teacher or has a child in the school. That is not bad, but it dilutes their representation of the more distal group that they were actually chosen to represent. Try to empower as many and as diverse a set of each group. A good example is student leaders. All too often, we give leadership roles and opportunities to the same star students over and over and do not offer them to the students who really need leadership experiences.

A specific aspect of sharing leadership is to look at school structures relevant to leadership, such as school committees. The use and nature of committees varies very widely, so it is difficult to generalize. I want to introduce two principles for thinking about committees. One is centrality and the other is inclusivity. If character education is truly to be a Priority, then the committee charged with leading the character education initiative in the school should be THE lead committee for the school. Many schools have a leadership committee of some sort and a "lesser" character education committee. Some have both of those plus other committees of relevance, such as a school climate committee. This tends to fractionate and dilute the priority of character education. Having one leading committee that is clearly focused on character, school climate, and school improvement is optimal. If indeed character education is the secret to school improvement overall, then your leading school committee should be charged with also focusing on character education. Remember, committees can have sub-committees with more specific foci.

I encountered an interesting empowerment failure a few years back when asked to do a breakout session on character education in a local school on one of their professional development days. I found myself in a room with about a dozen educators all from the same middle school. The administrators were apparently roaming the school sampling the various sessions and discussions. When one of the administrators was in the room, I asked the participants, "If you could subtract one thing from this school that would not be missed and would actually improve the school, what would it be?" Surprisingly there was a strong consensus around their committee structure. Apparently, all staff had to be on a committee and there was a designated day of the week when all committees met after school to do their work. They argued that most of those meetings were wasted time and they could use that time more productively if they were not forced to meet in unproductive meetings. Their leader heard it all but never spoke up and simply got up and left the room, assumedly to sample another discussion. Apparently, this idea was never addressed in the school, in particular by this administrator. This was both a failure of leadership and a waste of a committee structure.

The inclusivity of the committees repeats what we have just discussed about empowerment of all and being sure that all groups are represented. If a school is small enough, the committee can be all the staff. Ridgewood Middle School never had a character education committee at all, despite being completely dedicated to character education as their path from failing to excellence. Instead, the character education committee was the entire staff, because it was so important to all of the school. Many schools are larger than that, so it is a good idea to use a representative democratic approach. Have each subgroup (teachers, support staff, students, parents, etc.) select their own representatives to the committee and create a structured way for them to communicate with their constituencies. They can both report at subgroup meetings and poll the subgroups to present their constituency's thoughts at the committee meeting.

● ● ● ● ●

Democratic Classrooms

Schools skew toward being benevolent dictatorships. That is, out of authentic care for children, the adults in the school take care of the children without giving them voice, autonomy, or power over what happens in the school, in particular to them. They make choices in the best interests of the child, but the key phrase here is, "they make choices." This is true at the classroom level as well. We need strategies for empowering students in classrooms, which at its core is making classrooms more democratic. There are so many ways to do this.

My favorite pedagogical way to do this is to utilize class meetings as a regular classroom method. Class meetings are times for the classroom community to sit in a circle to engage in egalitarian discussions of a variety of topics and for a variety of purposes. An excellent description of how to do this is a small book called *Ways We Want Our Class to Be*, by the Developmental Studies Center (now renamed the Center for the Collaborative Classroom). It presents both techniques for class meetings and varieties of class meetings—for example, problem-solving meetings, check-in meetings, and decision-making meetings. In fact, on our center's website is a repository of some of the videos that accompany this book showing actual class meetings (https://chara cterandcitizenship.org/resources-title/video-galleries/cdp-videos). Other programs also emphasize class meetings and provide support for them; for example, the Responsive Classroom has an excellent class meeting model—called The Morning Meeting—and instructional book, *The Morning Meeting Book* by Roxann Kriete.

An important offshoot of this is empowering students to make the classroom rules. We tend to take better care of our own "stuff" than we do of others' "stuff." When kids make the rules, they are more likely to care about and follow them. I encourage all teachers to use class meetings at the beginning of the year to reflect on "how they want people to treat each other and behave" in the class and to generate a set of guidelines or rules about what people *should* do, rather than what they *should not* do. Then be sure those are learned, posted, and revisited periodically, often in subsequent class meetings. To see this powerfully in action, watch the two videos "September" and "Teasing" at our Center's website listed in the previous paragraph. "September" shows a three-day process of making the rules, and "Teasing" shows a mid-year check-in by the same class on how those same rules are functioning, which leads to a problem-solving meeting.

Another way to democratize a classroom is to engage in more student-led structures. Student-led parent—teacher conferences are a great way to empower students. Student-led project-based learning in general—and service learning in particular—are other ways of letting students take the lead in their own learning. Simply running a classroom where students make collective and individual decisions, where students are equipped and empowered to solve problems, and where learning is made relevant by allowing students' interests to steer the curriculum are all great ways to democratize a classroom. Because we discuss behavior management and discipline in other sections, we will not discuss it here, but it is clearly another area for empowerment in and outside of the classroom.

●●●●●

Culture of Empowerment/Collaboration

Since character education is a "way of being," empowerment needs to be thought of in that way too. Is the school generally an empowering place? Is there an authentic and pervasive culture of collaboration across all sectors and members of the school community? Do we collaborate frequently and meaningfully? When members of the school community spontaneously voice an interest in a project or issue, are they welcomed to partner/join despite their "status" in the school and connection to the topic?

These are great questions to ask yourself. More importantly, since we are talking about collaboration and empowerment, these are great questions to discuss at all levels and with all stakeholders of the school community. Find out if people regularly feel that their voices are welcome.

Organizational culture starts with the leader. What the leader models goes a long way in establishing the culture. This is as true of the leader of the whole school for all members of the school as it is for the leader of the classroom for all members of the classroom. So how can the leader model empowerment? One great way is through staff meetings. Sadly, so many staff meetings are boring, counterproductive for adult culture, and model terrible pedagogy. Moreover, they model hierarchical authoritarian leadership and stagnant didactic pedagogy. Years ago, I was asked to offer professional development for the staff at Abe Lincoln Elementary School in Belleville, Illinois on class meetings. About two or three weeks later, I received a call from the principal, Renee Goodman, telling me that when she arrived to set up the room for their next staff meeting, she discovered that a group of teachers had intentionally arrived before her to set the room up for a class meeting in a circle. Being an empowering leader, Renee followed their lead. She had called to tell me about it and particularly to tell me that it was the best faculty meeting they had ever had. No one wanted to end it, and, as a result, she was late to meet with the superintendent, Matt Klosterman. Matt fully understood, as this was not only a National School of Character, but the district was a National District of Character. They continued this empowering and successful way of "being" as a faculty.

I think faculty meetings should always be a class meeting type format. Sit in a circle. Perhaps discuss the same question every single time. . . . "How can we make this a better place for everybody?"

Another simple strategy for creating a culture of collaboration and empowerment is to shift systematically from giving answers to asking questions. A very simple technique is that when someone asks you a question, rather than answer it immediately, ask, "Why do you think. . . ?" or "What do you think. . . ?" For example, if a frustrated colleague asks the principal, "How can we get people to stop being so negative?" ask them, "How do you think we can get people to stop being so negative?" Or if a student asks you, "Should I put pictures and graphs in my paper?" ask them, "Do you think you should put them in the paper?" It is simple, but it shifts the "way of being" in the school. Moreover, it respects and elicits voice.

We try to get the leaders in our Leadership Academies to engage in collaborative leadership by giving them written assignments to be crafted, written, and assembled by a representative team of stakeholders. Many of them resist that and actually make the work more onerous and less beneficial by doing it all themselves. The irony is that we end up trying to drag those authoritarian resisters kicking and screaming into the wonderful world of collaboration, and they make their lives harder by resisting.

Finally, do a group study of the nature and benefits of teamwork and collaboration.

●●●●●

Fair and Respectful of Students

Almost all schools that have a core list of virtues or values include respect as one of them. And many have another having to do with justice or fairness. If these are indeed core values of character education, then it behooves us to treat people that way. How then can we treat students fairly and respectfully?

We have already discussed this in a variety of ways. We need to be aware of adultism and avoid treating students as less competent than they are, that is, of being motivated by a prejudice that tells us children need to be treated paternalistically and maternalistically in ways that are not only not true and necessary but actually disempowering and developmentally counterproductive. We need instead to give them voice in the ways we have already described and many more. We also need to institute just discipline systems such as we discussed in the section on Intrinsic Motivation and will revisit in the section on the final Design Principle, Developmental Pedagogy. In other words, we need to align the way we manage behavior with our central purpose (Prioritization) of schools that educate and nurture the flourishing of human goodness in our students.

Adults and school structures that disempower students are working counter to the fair and respectful treatment of students. They also poison the overall culture of the school. Respect and fairness are ways to demonstrate the authenticity of your caring.

Students are magnets for perceived injustice and disrespect, especially once they get past the early primary grades (approximately ages three through seven). Perhaps the most frequent lament by children in schools (and homes for that matter) is, "It's not fair!" If they tend to over-perceive injustice, then it behooves us to be especially vigilant about minimizing their opportunities to do so. Empowering them to be co-authors of their educational experiences is a great way to accomplish this. After all, it is much easier to oppose or be cynical about someone else's ideas or decisions than about ones that you co-created.

We have now explored the nature of, justification for, and best practices of each of the first five Design Principles of PRIMED. Look at the following Empowerment reflection sheet. And when you are done using it, ideally in a group process, it is time to tackle the sixth and final Design Principle: Developmental Pedagogy.

● ● ● ● ●

Resources

Publications

Developmental Studies Center (1996). *Ways We Want Our Class to Be*. Alameda, CA: Center for the Collaborative Classroom.
Kriete, R. (2014). *The Morning Meeting Book*. Turners Falls, MA: Center for Responsive Schools.
Parker, W. (2005). Teaching against idiocy. *Phi Delta Kappan*, 86(5).

Electronic Resources

Center for Character and Citizenship video gallery—https://characterandcitizenship.org/resources-title/video-galleries/cdp-videos
Center for Self-Determination Theory—www.selfdeterminationtheory.org

PRIMED Action Planning Worksheet:

Empowerment Strategies

Empowerment: Sharing power with all stakeholders but especially students. Creating structures, time, and processes for voices to be heard and to matter in the life of the school in meaningful ways. Increasing the democratic nature of the classroom/school/district.

Evidence-based implementation strategies:

Shared leadership

Democratic classrooms

Culture of empowerment/collaboration

Fair and respectful of students

STEP ONE:

Please identify at least two Empowerment strategies that are already in place in your school/district. You may use the previous categories or anything else you do that you think increases the degree to which power is shared and voices are welcomed and heard.

1.

2.

3.

4.

STEP TWO:

Please identify at least two more things you can do that would increase empowerment in your school/district. Again, you can choose from the previous list or list anything else you think would be good for you to implement for the purpose of increased democracy, sharing of power, and welcoming of and listening to voices.

1.

2.

3.

4.

Part VII

PRIMED Principle 6:
Developmental Pedagogy

21

●●●●●

Developmental Perspective: Thinking Long-term

Before we begin our exploration of taking a Developmental Perspective on education in general and character education in particular, it may be helpful to remember that the Six Design Principles of PRIMED tend to overlap. Most obviously, Prioritization not only refers to prioritizing character education in general, but it also means prioritizing each of the other five Design Principles. However, there are many more areas of overlap. Modeling and Relationship are foundational to nurturing Intrinsic Motivation. Developmental Pedagogy, as we will see in this section, shares many of the implementation strategies of Intrinsic Motivation. And so on. Now that all the other Design Principles have been put in play, we will see even more overlap in this section on Developmental Pedagogy. Therefore, do not be surprised to see examples from other Design Principles resurface in our discussion of Developmental Pedagogy.

When I first began studying human development, I learned it largely through the lens of constructivist theory, which at its center identified various stages of development. In my case, the focus was Lawrence Kohlberg's identification of six stages of moral reasoning development. As we move through life, our capacity to reason effectively and logically about moral issues transforms in regular ways from one stage to the next, each more complex and more capable of solving moral problems. My eye was always on which stage a particular person "was at." This was always based on Jean Piaget's more general theory of stages of cognitive development. The bottom line is that I—and others who worked in this same framework—saw human development through a lens of a series of static states of being. Almost like a herky-jerky climb up the staircase of life.

There is a wonderful scene in Herman Hesse's book *Siddhartha*, where Siddhartha finds a river that imparts to him the understanding of life's complexity, unity, and fluidity. For him, this is true enlightenment, to which he dedicates his life including teaching it to others. Similarly, a Developmental Perspective entails the understanding that every child who crosses our educational paths is an illusion of stability. Where a child is at this moment is really a part of a continuous and hopefully long life journey. If we think of this child as Siddhartha's river, then what we encounter is merely a small part of that life as it passes us when we are the child's teacher. To truly understand the child, we need to know both where the child came from and where the child is heading, to understand the river before it reaches us and where it goes down stream. Moreover, we need to understand that we will inevitably make ripples, will change the course of the stream, for better or worse.

Erik Erikson takes this idea of nurturing children for the long run even further. When he describes the fundamental psychological challenge of early adulthood as trying to establish a mature intimate relationship with a partner, he ends his long and brilliant definition of ideal intimacy (which for him is lifelong and procreative) with the admonition that it should "secure to the offspring, too, all the stages of a healthy development." What he is arguing is that when we bring children into the world, we have a moral obligation to educate toward their optimal lifelong development, not just now when they are little but for their entire lives. In a moment, we will explore the notion of developmental love that dovetails perfectly with Erikson's prescription.

Developmental Pedagogy is a perspective built around this understanding. It frames how we do education with an eye toward the long view. It is trying to understand why the child is the way she is now and trying to design and implement education to serve the long-term development and learning of the child. As we look at our students, we should see their current development and learning as road marks or waypoints on their lives' journeys and not as destinations. Whether they manifest a deeper understanding of honesty or a new commitment to personal responsibility or demonstrate a new mathematical or grammatical competence, we can rejoice in this but need to view it as part of a much longer and larger developmental journey. We must educate for the journey, not the specific destination alone, while always being sensitive to where the child is now.

One example of this perspective on education is the argument for relying on behavioristic approaches with younger kids or with kids with substantial behavior problems. The argument often invoked for the younger ones is that focusing on consequences of behavior is developmentally where they are. It is true that preschoolers and early primary grade students tend to understand right and wrong through a lens of concrete consequences, mostly to themselves. That is, something is wrong if a bad thing results and something is good if a good thing results. Hence, the focus on reward and punishment as aligned with how the kids themselves already and naturally understand the world.

However, this is ignoring the Developmental Perspective and enacting a non-Developmental Pedagogy. From a static perspective, we should treat kids where they are. From a Developmental Perspective, we should try to support them in moving to the next "waypoint" on their developmental journeys. What can we do to get them to be more sensitive to the feelings of others (cultivating empathy and sympathy) and the impact of their behaviors on the health of relationships? These, after all, are the next waypoints on their developmental journeys. Richard Weissbourd, director of Making Caring Common at the Harvard Graduate School of Education, urges us to educate toward "widening circles of concern," expanding the child's perspective from me to we to all of us. That is looking downstream to where they will journey next and designing our Developmental Pedagogy accordingly.

I am not arguing that knowledge of where kids are now is not helpful. It is. However, it needs to be wedded to an understanding of where they are heading—or rather where we hope they are heading. The Russian psychologist, Lev Vygotsky, described the Zone of Proximal Development (ZPD), which is a space in one's developmental journey where next steps are first developed. The idea is that as we are moving to new levels of mastery or understanding, we slowly play with aspects of them and master them in steps and pieces. Educators have long tried to create educational spaces that allow for such ZPD play and mastery. This is done with a focal eye on that developmental journey from current stage to next growth.

Another way to think about continual change is that life and development are fragile. Ideally, change is developmental, for the better. It is positive growth. That, however, is not guaranteed. We can see an analogy to focusing on individual development to analyzing organizational development. I learned from years of mentoring school leaders through school improvement and change that excellence is fragile. This is the crux of Jim Collins' book *Good to Great*, about organizational change. It is rare to see excellence attained and rarer to see it sustained. Sadly, few schools achieve true comprehensive (character and learning) excellence. Those that do typically do not sustain it for long, especially when there is a change of leadership.

One lesson from this and from a Developmental Perspective is to avoid complacency. If life is a journey and we want the journey to be toward progress, then we cannot be complacent, for complacency is the enemy of progress and the foundation of apathy. Embracing the fragility of the moment is one way to avoid complacency and to embrace a Developmental Perspective. While understanding that excellence is elusive and fragile, we should nonetheless set our bar high. High expectations, with appropriate supports or scaffolding, is one of the most established research findings in support of child development and learning, both in families and in schools. Another of the aphorisms we have encountered already is to always aim toward perfection but never expect it. We want high aspirations, but we set ourselves up for failure if we expect to achieve perfection.

Another caveat about a Developmental Perspective hearkens back to my earlier musings about being a long-term optimist. It was retired Principal BR Rhoads who ingrained in me that "children do not develop in straight lines." Nor do schools. The journey down the river is not without side eddies and rough water. It is not all smooth sailing. Lives, like rivers, tend to bend and even meander. If we think long-term however, then we can see the overall direction of learning and development. That is another important aspect of a Developmental Perspective; namely, that we often have to look long term to see the positive impact of what we do for children's learning and development. That is why, as we saw in the section on Intrinsic Motivation, our behavioral goals should be for the long-term enduring positive change in the child and not merely momentary cessation of the undesirable behavior. It is why we often do not know the profound impacts (both positive and negative) that we have on children's lives. It is also why we cherish those rare moments when we do hear from former students about the way we enriched and altered their lives.

To close this reflection on a Developmental Perspective, I want to introduce one of my favorite but little known and little understood concepts: Developmental Love. More than 40 years ago, I heard the philosopher Bill Puka introduce this concept. I found it so novel, important, and influential that I never forgot it, even though I have never heard anyone else talk about it since, including Bill.

There are many kinds of love, platonic friendship, romantic love, love of parents, love of a child, etc. Developmental love is loving someone by serving their best developmental interests. Loving by supporting and nurturing their journeys to become their best selves. It may not be doing what they most want—nor what will bring them pleasure. It is certainly not doing what is easiest or most expedient. But is it what will support their long-term (Developmental) flourishing. If we go back to the P in PRIMED, we can think of this in part as helping them discover and fulfill their Noble Purposes. Moreover, it is a form of servant leadership.

For many educators, like Esther Abramson to whom this book is dedicated, this is what they already do. However, for most educators it is a different *way of being*. It is *being* in a way that optimally serves the developmental journey of the child. Someday that child will be an adult, upon whom you have left your mark. Remember, the origin of the word "character" is to leave a mark on something or someone. Can you teach, can you *be*, in a way that is fully dedicated to leaving an enduring positive and developmental mark on the child? Can you put them on the best course in their life journeys, with an eye far downstream? That is a Developmental Perspective.

Now that we have explored the notion of taking a Developmental Perspective, it is time to turn to a consideration of how it can inform our pedagogical practice. That is what we mean by Developmental Pedagogy.

22

•••••

Developmental Pedagogy: Educating for the Long Run

Let us now take a closer look at some of the evidence-based strategies for educating for character development—or what we call Developmental Pedagogy. In our review of the evidence base, we identified three clusters of such implementation strategies: (1) simply direct teaching; (2) focusing on expectations for development or growth; (3) opportunities and structures to practice newly developing competencies and act on newly recognized motivations.

•••••

Direct Teaching of Character

The direct teaching of character has three sides to it: (1) teaching about character; (2) teaching character competencies; (3) integrating character education into the academic curriculum.

Once again, when Tom Lickona addresses the importance of role modeling, he often points that modeling character should be linked to teaching about character, "Practice what you preach, but don't forget to preach what you practice." Part of this is making lessons about character explicit, for people often do not derive the intended lesson just from observing a role model. They may misconstrue the motives of the actor or not understand the more distal outcomes of the modeled behavior, for instance. It behooves us to explain our inner workings such as our motives, assumptions, and knowledge.

Teaching about character must go beyond simply explaining our own behavior or that of others to include explanations of all character. At first blush, this should be the low-hanging fruit of character education. After all, if the professional competencies of educators have a center it would be "teaching about." Throughout the history of educating for character, didactic teaching has been front and center. It has an important place. Children need to be taught what is right and wrong. They need to understand the character concepts that may be core to a school's vision and character education initiative. If a school is committed to educating for character development, then it is likely that it has a set of prominent concepts (words, values, virtues, character strengths). They are a Priority. Implementing pedagogical strategies that help children recognize and understand them is a good foundational practice. Being sure they understand them deeply is just as important.

There are character education curricula and programs aplenty that one could choose from for that purpose, such as the Virtues Project. But if students graduate from our schools knowing those words, being able to spell and define them, showing proficiency in using them correctly in writing and speech, and even able to craft persuasive essays and speeches about them but not truly internalizing them or caring about them (Intrinsic Motivation), we have fallen far short of the mark of nurturing the flourishing of human goodness.

Character lessons are an important part of character education, but they are far from enough. All too many schools and educators act as if identifying such core concepts, posting them on the walls of the school, and proclaiming them to the heavens will be sufficient to achieve the goals of character education. They will not. Therefore, we need to look more deeply at how we teach character.

One important way to do this comes from the Head, Heart and Hand triumvirate of character. Teaching *about* mostly focuses on the Head. However, it leaves out the hand, the action part of character. We will focus on teaching to the hand throughout much of the rest of this chapter. However, here, under the subject of "teaching about character," I want to focus on one aspect of teaching to the hand, namely, teaching character skills.

The best locus of practices, structures, and supports for teaching character skills is the field of social-emotional learning or SEL (www.casel.org). For about three decades CASEL has been creating, implementing, and testing a wide array of lessons, curricula, and programs to teach children the core social-emotional competencies of self-knowledge and management, understanding others and managing relationships, and developing responsible decision making, all of which are foundational to the capacity ("the hand") to be an agent of good in the world. The set of resources from SEL is so vast that it is far beyond the scope of this discussion. Fortunately, CASEL has made them readily available on its website, along with many other supports for examining, evaluating, and adopting them.

However, one does not need to adopt a program or curriculum for this. Teachers all over the world spontaneously leverage teachable moments to help students discover and practice the "hand" of character, whether it is calming oneself down, paying attention, smiling at others, disagreeing agreeably, or any other character skill. Other times these are relegated to the curriculum taught by specialists such as guidance counselors, social workers, or special educators. They tend to be very good at that. But given that these are fundamental social, emotional, and moral competencies that all human beings need, I recommend that they are taught by the adults with whom students are closest and with whom they spend the most time in school: Their classroom teachers. In fact, those specialists can, instead of being asked to teach them directly, be a resource to help the classroom teachers learn the what and how of teaching this material.

Planned lessons are not the only way to do this. In fact, the first time Hal Urban taught his students how to greet others, it was not planned. He had assumed greeting them at the classroom door would be easy and go smoothly. He was caught off guard by how uncomfortable and ineffective most of them were at greeting him. Like all excellent educators, he saw a problem as an opportunity to teach . . . that is, as a teachable moment. He improvised a class lesson about the elements of successful greetings, which then became a mainstay of the start of every class he taught for over three decades.

As we have seen in the section on Intrinsic Motivation, Marilyn Watson's third principle of developmental discipline is to see misbehaviors as opportunities to teach. Rather than seeing them as opportunities to oppress, punish, torture, scar, or exact revenge on students, she urges educators to recognize that they are educators and not prison guards. They should opt instead for teaching students what they do not know or cannot yet do as a way of getting them to internalize character, which is a form of Developmental Pedagogy, as it supports their long-term character growth.

We have examined how to teach about character in general as well as how to teach character competencies. The final piece of the direct teaching of character is about how to teach character specifically within the academic curriculum. This actually goes a bit further than direct teaching of character, because the academic curriculum can be used for both direct teaching as well as the indirect nurturing of character growth through one's academic pedagogy. We will cover both here.

I make a distinction between academic integration of character education and what I call "wedging." The former is about leveraging the academic curriculum to add or highlight aspects of character education. For instance, we might focus in our literature on the ubiquitous themes of character in what we are reading. Alternatively, we might highlight the ethical quandaries uncovered in the study of environmental science or the motives and actions of protagonists in the study of history.

Wedging on the other hand is simply inserting character lessons at points in the school day. Both are useful ways to teach about character, but here we are concerned about how to integrate character into the academic curriculum. In doing so, it is important to organize our thinking in two clusters: (1) the content of the curriculum; (2) the academic methods we choose to teach that content.

When considering the content of our academic curricula, it is helpful to recognize a few facts.

- Almost all academic curricula are rife with character content and opportunities to highlight issues about or relevant to character. Nearly every piece of literature we read has issues of character, often seated in the motives and actions of the characters in literature. History similarly provides a nearly endless stream of events, historical figures, choices, and dilemmas that offer excellent opportunities to reflect on character. The scientific method and environmental studies in science fit perfectly here. In the arts, one can easily examine the values, messages, and motives of artists or specific pieces of art. Think of the curriculum as a mine, laden with lodes and nuggets of character. Educators simply need to don a miner's hat and direct the beam of light onto the nuggets and gems in the mine. When there are choices such as writing prompts or reading comprehension questions or group discussion topics, simply focus on the gems of character.
- Students love to talk about character. Discussing what is right or wrong and how people rise above or stumble in challenging situations are naturally attractive to students. This is partly because they are relevant to them, and relevance is one of the new three Rs of education: Rigor, relevance, relationships.
- If we focus on character within the curriculum, we do not need to wedge in character lessons. We often get push back from educators about doing character education more intentionally and comprehensively because they argue, "there is no more room on my plate." The character educator's reply is that "character education is not another thing on your plate. It is the plate." Mining the character content in your curriculum is a perfect example of this. You do not need to add character lessons if you highlight the character in your curriculum.
- If one does, however, want to adopt a new curriculum, there are academically excellent curricula available, usually in literature, that both promote academic achievement and focus on character. A good example is Making Meaning from the Center for the Collaborative Classroom.

While content is the most obvious part of one's curriculum, methods are critical to character education too. We have known this since research on some methods not specifically designed for character education have shown profound effects on character. There are many educational methods that have a beneficial effect on fostering character development.

A great example is cooperative learning. David and Roger Johnson have spent many decades at the Cooperative Learning Institute at the University of Minnesota looking at the research on cooperative learning and have found that it not only enhances academic achievement, but it also nurtures the flourishing of human goodness. Cooperative learning is essentially a form of experiential learning and therefore has the basic experiential learning structure of preparation, activity, and reflection.

The Center for the Collaborative Classroom, in its book *Blueprints for a Collaborative Classroom*, has offered many structures for such cooperative learning activities and have some general ways of turbocharging this important pedagogical strategy for greater character development. They simply add a few minutes to the preparation and reflection phases of cooperative learning. Rather than simply presenting and discussing learning goals in the preparation phase, they also present and discuss "social goals" such as listening, sharing, or turn-taking, goals that are specific to the cooperative activity to be done in the lesson. Students are asked to think about what might go awry and how they could avoid or repair such bumps in the social fabric of the lesson. Then when the learning activity is done and the post-activity reflection starts, they not only reflect on the academic learning but also reflect on their social goals and how they handled the social challenges of, for example, sharing the materials fairly or listening respectfully. In this way, social development is more focally nurtured and character developed more deeply.

I recommend doing an inventory of your curriculum. This is a great way to get all of the academic staff involved and feeling ownership. This can be done in academic department teams, in grade level teams, or in other groupings or even as a whole staff. Try to identify every opportunity to discuss or otherwise focus on character in your existing curriculum. Map it. Then you can turn to your lesson plans and update them, or write new ones if necessary, to capitalize on the gems of character already in your curricular mine.

I also recommend changing the templates you use for writing lesson plans. You could consider adding two lines at the top of the lesson plan: (1) character Content; (2) character Methods. Then—and only when it is appropriate because I am not arguing that all lessons need to cover character—annotate what character content is covered in that lesson and which character methods are employed to teach it.

Another great way to highlight character is through the school library. Librarians or media specialists usually love to bring their expertise to apply in this way. Some schools catalog their books and other holdings by the character content within them. For instance, if your school has five core values, then the librarian could color code each book according to which value or values it covers. This helps teachers in assigning books and helps students select books for their assignments—or even for their personal character journeys—something we will cover in detail in the following section.

●●●●●

Four Approaches for Expectations for Growth

In this section, we will talk about three approaches to nurturing character development through expectations for growth: (1) setting high expectations or focusing on excellence; (2) character as a self-project; (3) mental contrasting with implementation intention or, more simply, WOOP.

(1) *High Expectations*. One of the more widely substantiated strategies for nurturing development, both by parents and by educators, is high expectations. Research demonstrates the powerful positive effects of having high expectations for children. There are four things to remember when considering setting high expectations. First, the expectations, while set high, need to be possible. We should not set the bar so high that the child has no reasonable possibility of meeting the expectation. We see this all too often where parents compare a child to an older sibling. It might be reasonable to compare your child to her sister who is three years older than her and a high achiever herself, if the comparison were to where the older sister was when at the younger sister's current age, not to where the sibling is with three more years of maturity behind it.

To buttress high expectations, we need to provide the supports necessary so the child has access to what she would need to meet the expectations. This should not be a "sink or swim" strategy. Rather it is what we often call a "scaffolded" strategy. We may do this by pointing our child to resources that might help provide a solution; e.g., did you look up the definitions of all the terms? Alternatively, we might provide internet access or other sources of information. Scaffolding does not mean doing the work for the child; rather it means creating the context and providing the resources needed for them to have a chance at completing the task.

Once we set and scaffold high expectations, we need to realize that setting such expectations is usually ineffective if you do not also monitor progress, effort, and performance. In other words, you should not tell your child or one of your students that you expect all top grades/marks on the next academic reporting period and then not check what grades they achieved. One of the underleveraged aspects of such monitoring is that it is more important to monitor effort than it is achievement. All too often, and schools are terrible at this, we simply use final products, such as grades/marks in school, as the metric for success and reward or punishment. Research tells us that monitoring and even rewarding effort is much more productive.

Finally, and this is an echo of our section on Modeling, you have to model the excellence you want to see in your students. Asking them pay attention when you do not, asking them to be punctual when you arrive late to class, and penalizing them for late submitted assignments when you hand back their papers well after the promised date all undercut the power of setting high expectations. Hal Urban had a sign in his classroom that said, "Why not your best?" and he told his students that he always came to class trying to give them his best as a teacher, so why would they not also try to do their best?

This applies to character as well as to academic schoolwork or athletic or artistic endeavors. While we are concerned here with the former, it is worth noting that seeking and perhaps attaining high expectations in any endeavor can be character building. In fact, this is precisely what we described as performance character at the beginning of this book.

A final word on high expectations hearkens back the previous discussion about teaching character competencies. One such competency is goal-setting skills. I need that skill, you need it, everyone does. Teach your students how to set goals, such as S.M.A.R.T. goals, and then ask them to set their goals high. S.M.A.R.T. goals are specific, measurable, achievable, relevant (or results-oriented), and time-bound. This also gives a structure for them to monitor their own progress, the next topic.

(2) *Self-project.* The second strategy for setting expectations for growth, after setting expectations high, is to make character development a self-project. By this, I mean to empower students to be the captains of their own character journeys. There have been a few attempts to support this approach. In the USA, one of the John Templeton Foundation's (JTF) earliest initiatives was the Laws of Life Essay program in which first high school students and later younger students were asked to select a virtue that they wanted to be the compass for their character journey and to write a persuasive essay about it. The Laws of Life essay project led to many variations by those who were supported later by JTF to utilize this approach. Maurice Elias at Rutgers University, a leading authority in social-emotional learning, developed a more comprehensive version of this for middle school students.

In the United Kingdom, David Lorimer expanded this notion into the Inspire/Aspire program, which centers on 10–16-year-old students developing a poster pastiche of projects about their selected virtue, including self-reflections and an essay about a role model of that virtue (www.inspiringpurpose.org). The Jubilee Centre for Character and Virtue at the University of Birmingham in England created a wide set of resources called "My Character" for students to use in setting goals and monitoring their progress in developing their character (www.jubileecentre.ac.uk/1631/character-education).

I suggest the following considerations for making students' character their own project.

- Identify a core set of virtues/values/character strengths to target. Usually you will use the ones the school or school district had adopted. However, consider allowing students to nominate others.
- Challenge students to consider them all and to select one that they most want to improve now.
- Create structures for them to use to define, study, practice, and evaluate their chosen concept, such as the resources described above from David Lorimer of Character Scotland and the Jubilee Centre for Character and Virtue. At the minimum, you could simply have them write a paper about this, as in the Laws of Life Essay program. Ideally, however, make it a multi-disciplinary yearlong project, where you find places in and alongside the curriculum for them to dive deeper into this process. Ask them to look for their virtue in the curriculum like literature and history; use it for writing prompts; keep a journal about where it appears throughout their education; etc. Give the structures for and opportunities to chronicle their successes and stumbles. Have them evaluate their progress periodically.
- Have students create a composite record of their journey. It can simply be a folder or a notebook. Or they could use the Inspire/Aspire poster template, which can be acquired on Pinterest.org. Alternatively, it might be a multi-media portfolio.
- Consider assigning "accountability buddies" where two students are paired to systematically keep each other on track. There is no need for them to be pursuing the same virtue. This is about process and not content.
- Ask them to make public presentations at the end of the year about their respective journeys.
- Ideally, make this a school-wide structure so all teachers and all students are part of it. Then each student would start a new journey/project each school year. Moreover, they could generate a portfolio of their cumulative character journey across all the years in your school.

Another way to Empower students to captain their own character journeys is student-led parent–teacher conferences. At least in the USA, it is common practice for there to be designated days when teachers meet with parents to discuss student progress at school. Some schools have cleverly asked students to not only be present but also essentially plan and run the meeting including reporting, explaining, and justifying their academic success or stumbles to their parents. Including character progress in these meetings is a great way to further nurture character development while empowering students to take the lead on that journey.

(3) The third and final suggestion for setting expectations for character has a rather challenging name. It is called *mental contrasting with implementation intention*. However, it is worth working your way past the challenging name; it is a powerful and relatively simple strategy. Luckily, it has an easy to remember pseudonym . . . WOOP (www.woopmylife.org). WOOP stands for wish, outcome, obstacles, plan. Merely imagining a desired outcome (e.g., being a better friend, losing weight, etc.) does not work and in fact often saps your energy toward the outcome and leads to poorer outcomes. WOOP describes instead some essential elements that have been shown to greatly increase the likelihood of successfully moving toward those outcomes. The main elements are to mentally picture the outcomes, envision obstacles that might impede your progress, and then to make concrete plans about how to proceed and particularly how to overcome the envisioned obstacles.

Thinking back to the "hand" of character and our previous discussion of teaching the competencies of character, it behooves us to teach students the specific skills of WOOP so they can not only set high expectations but also have a good chance of reaching or at least approaching those expectations.

● ● ● ● ●

Practicing Character

It should not come as a shock that one important part of developmental, that is positive, change is practice. Just as one does not improve or develop in a sport or other physical skill without practicing it, so we are far less likely to improve our character without practice. Principle 5 of the Character.org *11 Principles Framework for Schools* is to provide "students with opportunities for moral action." There is great synergy between many of the strategies within Developmental Pedagogy, across the Design Principles, and with the *11 Principles Framework for Schools*. It is therefore not surprising that Principle 5 includes setting expectations, "The school sets clear expectations for students to engage in moral action."

One part of this is simply providing many opportunities to serve others, again as Character.org notes, "both inside and outside the school." This can be community service, service learning, peer tutoring, and many other ways of serving the needs of others and the greater good.

Developmentally, there are many theories and models of the need for practice. Jean Piaget described "practice/play" as a natural tendency of humans to practice and master new competencies by playing with them when they first emerge, like a baby loving to play "peek a boo" when she is discovering that people exist even when they are out of sight. Lev Vygotsky, as described earlier, introduced the Zone of Proximal Development, where children play with sub-skills as they work to master a more complex competency. It is natural for humans to spontaneously play and practice to serve mastery. However, it is wise for educators to institutionalize this natural tendency by being strategic and intentional and structural about it.

I know no better example of this than Ron Berger's pedagogy of excellence, eventually institutionalized in the work of Expeditionary Learning Schools (now ELEducation. org) where he is a leader. When still an elementary school teacher in rural Massachusetts, Ron intuited and created a pedagogy to instill *An Ethic of Excellence* (also the name of his book chronicling this journey). It is simultaneously simple and brilliant, easy and revolutionary. This discussion of Ron and ELEducation's work in this area could just as well have been included in the previous section on expectations, another example of the overlaps within the specific elements of Developmental Pedagogy.

Ron is not only an educator but also a carpenter. He realized that to be a useful carpenter one had to have an ethic of craftsmanship; that is; one had to have internalized (Intrinsic Motivation) an ethic of excellent work, the core of performance character. He then wondered if he could instill in his elementary school students the same ethic in regard to their schoolwork. Therefore, he set out to create a pedagogical approach to do just that.

It is beyond the scope of this book to detail all of what he figured out, designed, and implemented, but I will provide a few key elements. First, high expectations. His goal was for every student to produce excellent work. He included ALL students, including those with serious learning deficits and other educational and psychological challenges. One way he did this was to collect and show students examples of excellence. Before they would begin a project, he would show them what an excellent outcome could look like. Perhaps it was a drawing, or a video, or a science project report, and usually it was the work of a former student. Hence, students would begin with a clear and concrete sense of an excellent outcome.

Second, he relied heavily on project-based learning. Students worked for weeks or months on many of the projects he gave them or that they suggested themselves. Sometimes it was individual work, but usually it was group work. They became deeply involved in and committed to these projects.

Third, he asked them to do many revisions of their work. Students would try a first draft and then with constructive critical feedback would revise it. And do it again and again. Eventually, they would achieve excellence. Of course, most educators will not have a situation where they can do that regularly, but it is an excellent model that can be modified based on your reality. Perhaps you can do only one or two such projects a year or only do one revision of each piece of work.

Fourth, in order for the feedback to help the revisions, he taught students the character competency of how to give constructive critical feedback, which has three characteristics: (1) be kind; (2) be specific; (3) be helpful. Here we can again see the overlap with teaching character competencies discussed earlier. A great depiction of this is the short video featuring Ron recreating such a lesson: Austin's Butterfly (see resources at the end of this section).

Fifth, he relied heavily on public performance of completed work. Students would show off their products regularly to each other and sometimes to others, even to experts in the community. Ron went so far as to ask local architects to give constructive feedback to his 11 and 12-year-old students when they were designing an underground home. In addition, his oldest students had to present a portfolio of the best work they did across all the grades of this elementary school to a community panel in order to graduate. We tend to set the bar higher when we know others will view it.

Together these simple but clever pedagogical strategies allowed students to achieve high expectations in part through pedagogical scaffolding of those expectations, a model of a Developmental Pedagogy.

We have now seen how taking a long-term Developmental Perspective on character formation will lead us to use strategies for a Developmental Pedagogy. These strategies are varied but necessary if we want to effectively and strategically shepherd the journey of each of our students to blossom into their best possible selves.

Now it is time to examine and use the sixth and last reflection sheet to do a deeper examination of how your educational context is faring in taking a Developmental Perspective. Then we will turn to some final thoughts to close out our journey through the Six Design Principles of PRIMED.

● ● ● ● ●

Developmental Pedagogy Resources

Print Resources

Berger, R. (2003). *An Ethic of Excellence: Building a Culture of Craftsmanship in Schools.* New Hampshire: Heineman.
Collins, J. (2001). *Good to Great: Why Some Companies Make the Leap and Others Don't.* New York: Harper-Collins.

Electronic Resources

Austin's Butterfly (from ELEducation.org)—https://modelsofexcellence.eleducation.org/resources/austins-butterfly
Collaborative for Academic, Social and Emotional Learning (CASEL)—www.casel.org
Cooperative Learning Institute—www.co-operation.org/
Inspiring Purpose—http://inspiringpurpose.org.uk/
Jubilee Center for Character and Virtue "My Character"—Projectwww.jubileecentre.ac.uk/1631/character-education
Making Caring Common—https://mcc.gse.harvard.edu/
Mental contrasting with implementation intention (WOOP)—www.woopmylife.org
Making Meaning—www.collaborativeclassroom.org/programs/making-meaning/
S.M.A.R.T. Goals—www.smartsheet.com/blog/essential-guide-writing-smart-goals
The Virtues Project—www.virtuesproject.com

PRIMED Action Planning Worksheet:

Developmental Pedagogy Strategies

Developmental Pedagogy: Explicitly focusing on the long-term development of character in students, rather than short-term behavior management or change. Strategic practices that foster development.

Evidence-based implementation strategies:

Teaching Character:	Teaching about character
	Teaching social-emotional (SEL) competencies
	Curricular integration
Expectations for growth:	High expectations/Focus on excellence
	Mental contrasting with implementation intention
Practice:	Role playing/practice

STEP ONE:

Please identify at least two Developmental strategies that are already in place in your school/district. You may use the previous categories or anything else you do that you think supports the long-term development of character in students.

1.

2.

3.

4.

STEP TWO:

Please identify at least two more things you can do that would nurture Development of character in your students. Again, you can choose from the previous list or list anything else you think would be good for you to implement for fostering long-term development of student character.

1.

2.

3.

4.

Part VIII

Final Thoughts

23

•••••

PRIMED for Character Education

If you have read the foregoing chapters in this book, you should now be PRIMED to design and to implement an evidence-based effective and comprehensive initiative to nurture the flourishing of human goodness—and likely academic success and the development of performance, civic, and intellectual character as well. Here is what I hope you have gained from reading this book.

First, from the opening section of the book, you should have a new, deep, and broad understanding of what character is, how it develops, and how schools can be a critical player in such development. You should also have a deeper understanding of both the necessity and inevitability of educating for character development.

Second, you should also know what PRIMED is overall; that is a set of six overlapping "design principles" to guide the construction of a comprehensive, evidence-based, and effective character education initiative. From the sections on each of the Six Design Principles of PRIMED, you should have a deep understanding of the nature, importance, and challenges of each of those principles.

Third, you should have discovered specific implementation strategies for each of the design principles. While it is beyond the scope of this book to teach how to implement these strategies, I hope you have gained enough understanding to choose which strategies you want to consider. Fourth, you have been provided with many links and references and other resources to help you learn more about the ones that catch your fancy.

Fifth, at the end of each of the six PRIMED Design Principles sections, you have been provided a worksheet that you can use to identify what you are already doing that aligns with each of the design principles. More importantly, it guides you to consider which ones you would like to add to your existing repertoire of implementation strategies. Or which you need to revise or deepen.

Sixth, throughout the book you have been introduced to a series of aphorisms or mantras that I find particularly useful in orienting myself toward exemplary character education, successful schooling in general, and, well, life itself. Hang onto the ones that work for you and use them to orient yourself as you face the inevitable challenges of educating for the flourishing of human goodness. And to reorient yourself when you inevitably take a misstep along this complex and challenging journey.

You have "met" many schools and educators, especially educational leaders, who resonate with this framework as a path forward to achieving their noble purpose of nurturing optimal development and learning for their students. PRIMED is a framework for creating classrooms and schools, which are places where educators and students want to be. Places where they fulfill the three core needs identified in Self-determination Theory: (1) connection and belonging; (2) a sense of empowerment and autonomy where their voices matter and are valued; and (3) a sense of competence that they have something of value to offer.

I am often astonished at educators' puzzlement over how schools that follow best practices of character education, that take seriously an evidence-based focus on promoting social-emotional learning, or that strategically respond to the three needs of Self-determination theory by creating autonomy-supportive educational environments ultimately lead to academic achievement. When people, students and adults, authentically want to be there because it is an inclusive, empowering, and responsive place where you feel that you are safe, you matter, and the people care about you and model what they want all of us to be, then you engage more, work harder, and learn more. It is this kind of educational world toward which PRIMED aims.

To close out this book, I will provide suggestions for how you should proceed in using what you gleaned from these pages. Because it is a set of Design Principles for comprehensive school improvement, the book and the PRIMED framework on which it is based are intended to be applied directly to designing changes in your pedagogical practice. It is intended to help you adjust your fundamental *way of being* as an educator.

Interestingly, others have found these very same Design Principles to be applicable in other ways. Businesses and other organizations have found them useful in rethinking and improving their organizational structures and practices. Individuals have found them useful as a basis for daily living, even to the point of using them as a daily meditation about personal growth. Here, however, we will be talking from the perspective of school improvement. I will leave it to you to figure out how best to apply it—and the set of aphorisms—to other spheres of life.

First, I hope you have already been using the six PRIMED worksheets. We have used them very successfully in various professional development situations around the world, in different languages. If you have not used them, please consider going back to them and using them now that you have finished the book.

Second, I strongly recommend that you both study PRIMED and use the worksheets collaboratively. I am a great proponent of collaborative leadership and collective study and action in schools. If you have not already, ask others in your school also to read the book. You can do this in a variety of ways:

- Once you finish the book, pass it on.
- Organize a book study with a set of colleagues, perhaps those who are charged with leading the character education initiative in your school. If you do not already have such a team, form one. I recommend that it be truly representative of all the stakeholders in the school and not just teachers and administrators. Invite a couple of parents, a couple of support staff, a couple of community members who are neither parents nor staff, and perhaps some students.
- Buy copies for the entire staff and use it for professional development and even your official School Improvement Plan.
- Simply copy the Reflection Sheets and ask colleagues to use them too, again ideally collaboratively.
- Be very deliberate about making strategic plans for specific implementation intentions, make them concrete and specific, write them down, and share them publicly. Perhaps use the WOOP model we discussed in the prior chapter.
- And generally, as you create or revise practices, structures and policies, ask yourself the six design questions:

  - How can we prioritize character development here?
  - How can we design and implement this more interactively with an eye on nurturing healthy relationships?
  - How can we get this stuff to go inside the students, to become the character toward which we are educating?

- Are we modeling what this policy or practice promotes? How can we do that better?
- How can this be done by sharing ownership and authorship more widely?
- How can we do this in a way that will carry students on the long journey of life?

Whatever you choose to do, please remember to keep your eye on the target. If the character development of your students is truly to be your noble purpose, then Prioritizing effective character education has to be authentic. This is both about the kids and about the future of the world. It is about individual development and it is about *Tikkun Olam* (healing the world). It is essential. It is unavoidable. And it is rocket science.

However, do not be daunted by this. It can be done and it has been done, both frequently and excellently as many of the examples in this book demonstrate. You can do it and you should do it. It is my fervent hope that the Six Design Principles of PRIMED and this book will help guide you on this noble path to healing the world by investing in nurturing the flourishing of human goodness in the children entrusted to our schools.